GACE

Special Education Adapted Curriculum Practice Questions

Mometrix
TEST PREPARATION

DEAR FUTURE EXAM SUCCESS STORY

First of all, **THANK YOU** for purchasing Mometrix study materials!

Second, congratulations! You are one of the few determined test-takers who are committed to doing whatever it takes to excel on your exam. **You have come to the right place.** We developed these practice tests with one goal in mind: to deliver you the best possible approximation of the questions you will see on test day.

Standardized testing is one of the biggest obstacles on your road to success, which only increases the importance of doing well in the high-pressure, high-stakes environment of test day. Your results on this test could have a significant impact on your future, and these practice tests will give you the repetitions you need to build your familiarity and confidence with the test content and format to help you achieve your full potential on test day.

Your success is our success

We would love to hear from you! If you would like to share the story of your exam success or if you have any questions or comments in regard to our products, please contact us at **800-673-8175** or **support@mometrix.com**.

Thanks again for your business and we wish you continued success!

Sincerely,
The Mometrix Test Preparation Team

Printed in the United States of America

TABLE OF CONTENTS

Practice Test #1

1. Introducing each of the stages of career development for students with disabilities should be determined most by which of the following?

a. The student's developmental level
b. The student's grade level in school
c. The student's level of experience
d. The student's chronological age

2. A kindergarten teacher has a new student who will not make eye contact with anyone, so she doesn't appear to be listening. She often rocks back and forth and does not stop when asked or give any indication she has heard. She avoids physical contact. Sometimes the teacher must take her arm to guide her from one place to another. Occasionally the student erupts, howling in terror and fury. The most likely diagnosis is:

a. Conduct Disorder
b. Obsessive-Compulsive Disorder
c. Autism
d. Oppositional Defiant Disorder

3. It is important to teach life skills to students with developmental delays to prepare them for life after school. Which of the following skill sets should these students be taught?

a. Counting money, planning meals, grocery shopping, recognizing safety concerns
b. Counting money, ordering delivery meals, dating, driving
c. Driving, styling and maintaining hygiene, socializing, dating
d. Investing in the stock market, hairdressing, house painting, taking care of pets

4. Andrea was transitioned from a residential facility for the individuals with developmental disabilities to a group home. Her medications contribute to bladder control problems. She was successfully trip-trained in toileting at the residential facility. After moving to her new home, she began having episodes of enuresis at night. What should her team do?

a. Reinstitute trip-training at the group home.
b. Search for another strategy in this setting.
c. Have her wear adult diapers to bed.
d. Have her wear absorbent underwear to bed.

5. Which statement is most likely to be true?

a. All teachers should do whatever is necessary to acquire basic knowledge of common symptoms of special needs in children, as well as typical interventions and strategies for instructing high-needs students.
b. Teachers are always the most equipped individuals to determine a child's individual needs and interventions; however, most schools require evaluation by a professional.
c. All children should be considered "high-needs;" teachers should teach each child as though he or she may have learning difficulties when instructing and guiding them.
d. Students with learning or physiological challenges are best served in separate classrooms, where they can get the specialized attention and services they deserve.

6. A four-year-old child has difficulty sorting plastic cubes, circles, and triangles by shape, doesn't recognize patterns easily, and doesn't understand the relationship between little/big, tall/short, many/few. The child enjoys counting but does not say the numbers in proper order nor recognize the meaning of different numbers. This child most likely:

a. Has dyspraxia
b. Is developing within an acceptable range
c. Has dysgraphia
d. Has dyscalculia

7. Verbal dyspraxia is:

a. A motor skill development disorder that includes trouble with the physical act of writing
b. A motor skill development disorder that includes refusal to speak
c. A motor skill development disorder that includes misplacing letters within words
d. A motor skill development disorder that includes inconsistent speech errors

8. Christopher is an eight-year-old boy with multiple disabilities, including profound intellectual disabilities, spastic quadriplegia, and right-sided vision and hearing impairments. Though wheelchair-bound, he is very active, traveling through the halls, visiting different classrooms, and moving on to other places. If he is not closely monitored, he will take off for parts unknown, and staff need to supervise him constantly to keep up with his activities. When not watched, he has chewed on countertops to the point of damaging them (as well as possibly his teeth). He is also quite capable of getting into dangerous or toxic substances, such as cleaning supplies. Staff members disagree: Some teachers and even one nurse believe that he has attention-deficit hyperactivity disorder (ADHD) and should be prescribed medication to reduce his peripatetic and sometimes destructive behaviors. Another nurse, the doctor, and the psychologist are not convinced of this. What is another likely explanation for Christopher's behavior?

a. His developmental level
b. A lack of proper training
c. An impulse control disorder
d. A non-stimulating environment

9. Melissa is an eighth-grade student who receives services as a student with autism spectrum disorder. Which of the following co-occurring conditions is Melissa LEAST likely to suffer from?

a. Anxiety
b. Epilepsy
c. Sleep conditions
d. Orthopedic impairments

10. Charles is a young man with a dual diagnosis of mental illness and mild intellectual disabilities. In the past, he lived for several years at a residential facility. Before his admission to this facility, Charles' behavior was difficult for teachers and caregivers to control. He had a history of stealing, running away, and hiding. However, after spending many years in a highly structured program at this facility, he was much improved. He was doing so well that he was placed into a group home in the community. Shortly after this placement, Charles ran away from the group home. He ended up homeless in the downtown area. A couple who worked at his former residential facility and who had been on good terms with Charles happened to spot him when they were downtown. They tried to speak to him, but he ran and hid. What is the most likely reason for Charles' behavior following his community placement?

a. Charles must not have liked the other residents or the new caregivers in the group home.
b. Charles must have needed the structured environment and regressed when deprived of it.
c. Charles must have preferred the residential facility's campus over the setting of the house.
d. Charles must not have been fully prepared for an effective transitioning program.

11. Dick has been living in a residential facility and is about to move into a home in the community. He has mild intellectual disabilities and multiple health problems. He is fairly high-functioning and has good personal care skills. He comes from a dysfunctional family background, having lived in a trailer with parents who were alcoholic, addicted to drugs, physically abusive, and reclusive. He never learned many life skills because of this. He has learned good personal hygiene and dressing skills at the facility. He is already very good at performing simple work activities. Which of these is an activity he may be working on now to prepare further for community living?

a. Preparing simple meals in a home-like setting with a teacher's guidance
b. Learning a variety of academic subjects in a classroom to further his education
c. Practicing how to sort hardware pieces in the facility's on-campus workshop
d. Practicing how to brush his teeth, wash his face, put on clothes, and tie his shoes

12. Mr. Shirley's student Billy has been told in the past that he will never accomplish anything because of his disabilities. Billy has potential but lacks confidence. Which of the following statements by Mr. Shirley is most likely to enhance Billy's motivation in school?

a. "It's okay, Billy. I know you're doing the best you can."
b. "Oh, come on now, Billy, you can do better than that!"
c. "Billy, I know you can do this. I'm counting on you!"
d. "Don't worry about it if it's too hard for you, Billy."

13. Debbie has Down syndrome with mild intellectual disabilities and has always lived at home with her parents. She is about to graduate from high school. She and her parents both want her to have a job in the community. Which of these would be most helpful for her teacher to do?

a. Contact a local community-based supported employment agency.
b. Search the employment want ads for jobs that Debbie could do.
c. Show Debbie how to search the employment want ads for jobs.
d. Show Debbie's parents how to apply for jobs on her behalf.

14. Ms. Loomis is a teacher of students with learning disabilities in Texas. This term she has had a new group of students referred to her for reading difficulties. She realizes that all these students are English language learners (ELLs). Which statement about these referrals is most likely to be true?

a. These students will have reading problems regardless of which language they are reading.
b. The language acquisition process may well be the cause of these students' reading problems.
c. These students' reading problems are most likely the result of their learning disabilities.
d. These students' reading problems and their ELL status are most likely a coincidence.

15. Which of the following is most likely to be true about students with learning disabilities and their families?

a. Families that have children with disabilities typically bond closer.
b. Parents can sometimes be the cause of a learning disability.
c. Parents will often suspect a disability before the school does.
d. Families often seek out information about disabilities.

16. Which of the following is an example of a fine motor skill that a four-year-old student would be expected to do?

a. Hop on one foot
b. Catch a ball
c. Cut with scissors
d. Ride a tricycle

17. Which of the following students would most likely require coordinated community-based services as part of their postsecondary transition goals?

a. Students with autism spectrum disorder
b. Students with emotional disturbances
c. Students with multiple disabilities
d. Students with traumatic brain injuries

18. Which of the following are children born with rubella NOT more likely to have?

a. Deafness
b. Paralysis
c. Blindness
d. Cataracts

19. Which of the following is the best example of a postsecondary transition goal for a student who wants to be a veterinarian?

a. Jimmy will go to college to study biology and animal science.
b. Jimmy will research the job requirements of a veterinarian.
c. Jimmy will become a veterinarian after graduation.
d. Jimmy will take classes in high school to prepare him to become a veterinarian.

20. Gordon is an 11th-grade student with an other health impairment and a postsecondary goal of attending college. Which of the following would likely be LEAST productive for Gordon as he seeks to achieve this goal?

a. Reaching out to colleges in the area to tell them about Gordon
b. Assisting Gordon in researching colleges he wants to attend
c. Helping Gordon to discover professions he may be interested in
d. Providing opportunities for Gordon to practice filling out applications

21. In teaching basic mathematics, the following actions by teachers will benefit all students. However, which one is most likely to be needed more specifically for students with special needs in a general education classroom?

a. Carefully planning the coverage and order of instructional math content
b. Judicious selection and application of the specific instructional strategies
c. Designing practice activities that take a wide range of student needs into account
d. Giving intensive, direct instruction in mathematics to individual students

22. What statement is true regarding literacy?

a. The same literacy skills in students apply across subjects
b. The literacy demands of society have changed over time
c. Literacy required of pupils stays constant across grades
d. Literacy is best taught in the schools in a separate lesson

23. Which classroom environment is most likely to support a student with attention-deficit/hyperactivity disorder (ADHD)?

a. Students with ADHD become bored easily, so a classroom with distinct areas for a multitude of activities will stimulate her. When she loses interest in one area, she can move to the next and continue learning.
b. Students with ADHD are highly aggressive and easily fall into depression. The teacher needs to provide a learning environment in which sharp objects such as scissors, tacks, or sharpened pencils are eliminated. This ensures greater safety for both student and teacher.
c. Students with ADHD are highly creative. A room with brightly colored mobiles, a multitude of visual and physical textures (such as striped rugs and fuzzy pillows) and plenty of art-based games will stimulate and encourage learning.
d. Students with ADHD are extremely sensitive to distractions. A learning environment in which visual and audio distractions have been eliminated is best. Low lighting, few posters, and a clean whiteboard help the student focus.

24. A resource teacher wants to design a lesson that will help first and second graders learn irregular sight words so all the students can read their lists. She should teach them how to:

a. Divide sight words into syllables. Considering one syllable at a time provides a sense of control and increases confidence.
b. Recognize word families. Organizing similar words allows patterns to emerge.
c. Sound out the words by vocalizing each letter. Using this approach, students will be able to sound out any sight word.
d. Memorize their lists by using techniques such as songs, mnemonic devices, and other fun activities. By definition, irregular sight words cannot be decoded but must be recognized on sight.

25. What can a teacher do in regard to the physical environment of the classroom to increase attention and learning?

a. Cover every wall with posters
b. Play music
c. Ensure the class is brightly lit
d. Arrange the desks in a circle

26. A classroom teacher has a student with learning disabilities that affect her ability to do math. The teacher consults with the special education teacher and decides she will modify the work the child is given by reducing the number of problems, letting her have extra time to finish, and providing her with a multiplication chart. Which of the following statements on the teacher's actions is accurate?

a. The teacher is giving the student an unfair advantage. Letting her have extra time should be sufficient.
b. The teacher is giving the student an unfair advantage. Providing a multiplication chart should be sufficient. With that, she should get her work done on time.
c. The teacher is making appropriate modifications. Each child is different. In this case, she consulted with the special education teacher and concluded the child needs multiple supports.
d. The teacher is modifying the student's work because it makes it easier on the teacher. There is less to explain and less to grade.

27. Part of the emotional environment of a classroom is the relationships between the teacher and the children. Children learn and develop well in a nurturing relationship that includes all the following EXCEPT:

a. Consistency in the teacher's interactions with and expectations of the children
b. A firm emphasis on compliance with rules and routines
c. The empowerment of children with choices
d. The delivery of feedback in a positive manner

28. Behavioral management should include specific techniques for students who have difficulty staying on task. Which one of the following would NOT be appropriate?

a. Allowing such students to walk around to look at the materials that pertain to the lesson
b. Assigning specific tasks to be completed
c. Using response cards so that all students feel compelled to be aware and involved
d. Not allowing peer helpers because they might harm more than help by distracting the students who have trouble staying on task

29. Which of the following statements is most true about adaptations teachers may need to use in testing, teaching, and materials to address the needs of individual students?

a. Some students use communication modes unfamiliar to the teacher.
b. Differentiation of instruction is unnecessary between boys and girls.
c. Teachers are unlikely to encounter age differences in the same class.
d. Students speaking other languages must quickly adapt to using English.

30. Derrick is a student with profound intellectual disabilities and cerebral palsy. He can only use one arm and hand. He cannot speak but has good receptive language skills. His eyesight is good and he is cooperative. His teacher, Sam, needs to write some career skills in Derrick's IEP. Which of these would be a potential job for Derrick, for which Sam can write learning objectives?

a. Assembly of small machine parts
b. Sorting of small machine parts
c. Assembly line work with machine parts
d. Requisitioning and ordering machine parts

31. Mr. Hunt is a special education teacher with an elementary school class. He has one teacher's aide, one paraprofessional, and one parent volunteer, a mother, in his classroom. He uses peer tutoring methods as well. Three students—Marc, Fran, and Joe—have physical disabilities requiring assistance with snack time, bathroom breaks, and arts and crafts projects. One student, Clarence, likes to work alone on his math problems, but it is very important to him to have an adult check his work when he is done. Another student, Misty, is also very independent in her writing and art projects, but she needs the emotional support of periodic encouragement on her progress and praise for her results when she is done. Daisy and Carmela are similar in age and educational level and are friends, but Daisy excels in math and is below grade level in reading, while Carmela reads above her grade level but is below grade level in math. Which scenario is an example of the best use of Mr. Hunt's human resources in his classroom?

a. The paraprofessional assists Marc, Fran, and Joe with snacks, bathroom breaks, and arts and crafts projects; the teacher's aide checks Clarence's work and reports to Mr. Hunt so Mr. Hunt can explain Clarence's errors to him and assign additional exercises; the parent volunteer encourages and praises Misty; and Daisy and Carmela take turns helping each other in math and reading.
b. The paraprofessional checks Clarence's work, explains his errors, and assigns additional exercises; the parent volunteer takes Marc, Fran, and Joe to the bathroom; the teacher's aide helps with snacks; Daisy and Carmela take turns encouraging and praising Misty; and Mr. Hunt helps Marc, Fran, and Joe with arts and crafts projects.
c. Mr. Hunt takes Marc, Fran, and Joe to the bathroom; the parent volunteer checks Clarence's work, explains his errors, and assigns him additional exercises, and she helps with snacks; the paraprofessional helps Daisy with her reading and helps Marc, Fran, and Joe with arts and crafts; and the teacher's aide helps Carmela with her math.
d. Mr. Hunt encourages and praises Misty; Mr. Hunt helps Marc, Fran, and Joe with arts and crafts and takes them to the bathroom; the teacher's aide helps Marc, Fran, and Joe with snacks; the paraprofessional helps Carmela with math and Daisy with reading; and the parent volunteer checks Clarence's work, explains his errors, and assigns him additional exercises.

32. Annie is a student with severe intellectual disabilities, a personality disorder, and a history of maladaptive behavior, including tantrums, self-injury, aggression, and property destruction. One day, behavioral staff members are on a field assignment and not present at the school when Annie has a major tantrum. A teacher reports the incident to them when they return. Which of the following would the staff likely have employed had they been there?

a. Proactive strategies during tantrum escalation
b. Reinforcement during tantrum escalation
c. Proactive strategies before the tantrum could escalate
d. Proactive strategies during the tension reduction phase

33. Bruce is a student who periodically has behavioral crises when his level of tension rises too high. His behavior assessment does not indicate that his episodes are attention-seeking. His behavior can become violent if it is not de-escalated, but he responds well to intervention and has only rarely ever hurt himself or others. Based on this information, what would be the most appropriate form of early crisis intervention for him?

a. Physical restraint
b. Mechanical restraint
c. Verbal de-escalation
d. Extinction (ignoring)

34. For students who are deaf from birth and use sign language, which of the following would an advocate of inclusion NOT consider an inclusive educational strategy?

a. Students attend a general education school and are pulled out for special instruction.
b. Students attend a regional or magnet school whose location requires living apart from their families.
c. All students and teachers in the general education school are taught to use sign language.
d. All classrooms having deaf students are assigned sign language interpreters.

35. Which of the following classroom arrangements would be most appropriate for active teaching and learning?

a. Traditional rows and columns
b. Horseshoe shape
c. Clusters
d. Runway seating

36. Which of the following is the best description of maintaining a previously learned skill?

a. Performing the skill in a variety of settings
b. Practicing the skill when it is learned
c. Progressing on the learned skill
d. Continuing to practice the learned skill

37. When teaching an eighth-grade class, which one of the following strategies in communicating with parents best promotes a safe classroom environment?

a. Sending home the list of class rules to the parents
b. Getting to know the background and interests of the parents
c. Ensuring that behavior issues are communicated to parents
d. Reporting positive student behavior to the parents

38. Which one of the following learning environments best allows for differentiated instruction?

a. Randomly placing the students with additional support needs throughout the classroom
b. Selectively placing the students with additional support needs throughout the classroom
c. Placing the students with additional support needs clustered together
d. Placing the students with additional support needs at the front of the class

39. How would the use of a supplementary curriculum be most appropriate for a group of high school students in a social studies class?

a. Providing the students with accommodations to access the curriculum
b. Providing the students opportunities to explore careers
c. Providing the students use of assistive technology
d. Providing the students extra credit for additional assignments

40. Which of the following would be the LEAST appropriate reason to provide a social skills intervention group for students?

a. To teach social problem solving
b. To teach behavioral skills
c. To decrease antisocial behaviors
d. To increase friendships

41. Jessie is a fourth-grade student with an emotional disturbance that seems to struggle with self-reflection. Which of the following behavior management models would be most likely to meet his needs?

a. Assertive discipline
b. Logical consequences
c. Reality therapy
d. Love and logic

42. Which of the following best describes how daily learning objectives can be implemented to assist students who are working on adaptive skills?

a. To teach students to learn how to complete a new task
b. To teach students to improve reading ability
c. To teach students to learn about organization
d. To teach students to improve basic math skills

43. Jeanine is a ninth-grade student who often disrupts class with outbursts when she doesn't get her way. Which of the following would be the LEAST effective way to respond to her behavior when this occurs?

a. Ignore the behavior and continue class
b. Calling for backup
c. Negotiating with her
d. Removing her from class

44. Anna is a fourth-grade student with a disability who is struggling with reading comprehension in her social studies class. Which of the following would be the best option for ensuring that Anna can appropriately access the general education curriculum?

a. Moving Anna to the third-grade social studies class
b. Reteaching the concepts in her special education class
c. Placing a paraprofessional in her social studies class
d. Modifying the content in her social studies class

45. Which of the following best supports differentiated instruction?

a. Lecturing in a clear voice and using simple language
b. Assigning the same essay to all students
c. Offering a choice of an essay, presentation, or video for the final project
d. Bringing in guest speakers of various nationalities

46. Why might it be difficult to incorporate different kinds of activities each day when teaching a class with students of varying disabilities?

a. Some students require structure in their daily routine.
b. Some students may not have the knowledge required for each activity.
c. Some students may not be comfortable working with other students.
d. Some students require specific activities in their IEPs.

47. For which group of students would it be most appropriate to implement a functional curriculum at the elementary school level?

a. Students with intellectual disabilities
b. Students with specific learning disabilities
c. Students with speech or language impairments
d. Students with developmental delays

48. Which of the following is the most correct statement about manipulatives for teaching math in grades K–12?

a. They are only efficacious when they are actual physical objects.
b. They help make an abstract subject more concrete for learners.
c. They are not yet available virtually on personal computers and so would not work.
d. They actively engage students less than traditional math classes.

49. In core activities to teach phonological awareness, what would typically be introduced the earliest?

a. Phoneme blending
b. Phoneme segmenting
c. Initial phoneme identification
d. Phoneme substitution

50. A resource room teacher has a small group of second and third graders who are struggling with reading comprehension. The most effective strategy would be to:

a. Present a list of vocabulary words before students read a particular text.
b. Ask students to create a play about the story.
c. Read a story aloud. Ask students to raise their hands when they hear an unfamiliar word.
d. Have each child keep a book of new vocabulary words. Whenever an unfamiliar word is seen or heard, the student should enter the word in this personal dictionary.

51. A kindergarten teacher is showing students the written alphabet. The teacher pronounces a phoneme, and one student points to it on the alphabet chart. The teacher is presenting:

a. Letter-sound correspondence
b. Rote memorization
c. Predictive analysis
d. Segmentation

52. Which of the following types of groups would be most beneficial for a low-achieving student?

a. Homogeneous group
b. Heterogeneous group
c. Achievement group
d. Learning group

53. Which of the following is NOT a good practice to incorporate for students who have difficulty finishing routine assignments?

a. The teacher should teach self-discipline for staying on task.
b. The teacher should avoid incorporating games into the materials because they might add too much time to the task.
c. The teacher should remove segments of the task, such as requiring the student to copy word problems before calculating the answer.
d. The teacher should divide the task into segments and allow the student to work on the parts throughout the day.

54. Which of the following is true regarding alternate curriculum programs?

a. These programs are the first choice for students identified with disabilities
b. A student's eligibility for these programs is determined by his/her IEP team
c. They are preferable to general curricula with accommodations/modifications
d. Students are primarily assigned to general education classrooms in these programs

55. Jenny is a student teacher majoring in special education. She is working with a small group of students who are six years old and have mild developmental delays. She wants to give them some Piagetian tasks to try. Which of these would be most appropriate?

a. Tasks involving conservation of numbers, using rows of the same number of pennies, pebbles, or beads, arranged different distances apart
b. Class inclusion tasks using pictures and a 20-questions game to figure out which one the teacher is thinking of
c. Tasks involving conservation of weight, using boxes filled with sand arranged differently (e.g., stacked or side by side)
d. Tasks involving conservation of volume, using liquid in differently shaped containers (e.g., a tall, skinny container and a short, wide container)

56. Gary is nonambulatory, blind, and has profound intellectual disabilities. He loves music. Gary can propel his wheelchair with his hands, but he has become so accustomed to having caregivers push his wheelchair that he relies on them and is not interested in propelling himself. Gary's multidisciplinary team members (behavior specialist, teachers, and direct caregivers) are working on an IEP objective for Gary to propel his wheelchair more of the time, with a goal of greater independence in mobility. Which of the following would be the best way to accomplish this?

a. Connect Gary's boom box to his chair so it plays music whenever his hands move the wheels.
b. Connect Gary's boom box to his chair so that it plays music whenever the wheels are turning.
c. Only allow Gary to hear music after he has wheeled his chair all the way down the hall.
d. Play music for Gary all the time, encourage him to wheel his chair, and praise him for it.

57. Which of the following is NOT a good example of adapting education to maximize the physical abilities of students with specialized needs?

a. Wyatt, who cannot write with a pen but can use his fists, answers test questions using a computer with a touch screen.
b. Fabian, who is blind and does not read Braille, listens to recorded test questions on a tape player with earphones, answering by pressing buttons on a counter.
c. Sue, who has impaired vision and impaired fine motor skills, takes a pen and paper test along with the rest of the students in her class.
d. Donnie, who is deaf, can participate in school fire drills because the school has both sound alarms and strobe lights.

58. Bart is not only graduating from elementary/middle school and entering high school; he is also being mainstreamed from a special education class and school to a general education class in a regular high school. All of his teachers, therapists, and other team members as well as his parents agree he has developed the skills needed to be successful in this new placement. Despite his accomplishments, Bart is very anxious about the move. What can his teacher do?

a. Recommend that he be medically evaluated for an anti-anxiety prescription medication.
b. Advise against the move until such time as his anxiety abates.
c. Teach Bart coping skills to help him to manage the transition.
d. Disregard his anxiety and move him; he will get over it.

59. Corey is a second-grade student who receives special education services due to a specific learning disability in the area of reading fluency. Which of the following is the best strategy for ensuring success for Corey if he is severely impacted by his reading fluency deficiencies?

a. Providing additional support in the classroom
b. Pulling Corey for small-group reading fluency intervention
c. Modifying the material that Corey is to complete
d. Pulling Corey for one-to-one reading fluency intervention

60. Which of the following intervention strategies would be most effective in assisting a student who struggles to learn vocabulary terms?

a. Providing the student with a multisensory model
b. Supplying visuals with the words
c. Creating frequent vocabulary quizzes
d. Allowing students to use a dictionary

61. Which of the following classroom climate factors is most important when working with at-risk learners with disabilities?

a. Allowing the students to access accommodations
b. Providing a caring classroom setting
c. Allowing these students to collaborate with peers
d. Providing opportunities for after-school activities

62. Which of the following is the best example of guided practice when supporting a fifth-grade general education social studies class with multiple students with disabilities?

a. Students independently complete a map worksheet.
b. Teachers provide feedback on the map worksheet.
c. Students work in small groups to complete the map worksheet.
d. Teachers model how to complete the map worksheet.

63. Jessica is a ninth-grade student who struggles with becoming distracted while she works in the general education setting. Which of the following methods of differentiated instruction would be most beneficial to Jessica?

a. Differentiating the learning environment
b. Differentiating the content
c. Differentiating the process
d. Differentiating the product

64. Which of the following instructional strategies is most appropriate in supporting the immediate transition of eighth-grade students into high school?

a. Researching professions that they may be interested in
b. Researching colleges that they may want to attend
c. Researching classes that the high school offers
d. Researching independent skills that they may need

65. Zachary is a 10th-grade student who receives special education services as a student with another health impairment due to his ADHD, and he struggles to sit still for long periods of time. Which of the following strategies would be most effective in providing opportunities for Zachary to move around?

a. Giving Zachary a pass to move around when he needs to
b. Giving Zachary a timer to get up and stretch every 10 minutes
c. Organizing the classroom so that Zachary has his own area
d. Incorporating movement activities for the entire class

66. Why is instructional scaffolding a useful strategy when teaching students with disabilities?

a. Students are provided an alternate method of learning the lesson.
b. Students are provided multisensory approaches to learning the lesson.
c. Students are provided additional support in learning the lesson.
d. Students are provided less instruction when learning the lesson.

67. Which of the following is an example of an early intervention service for a student who is being evaluated for a developmental disability?

a. Speech services
b. Academic services
c. Counseling services
d. Adaptive services

68. Courtney is an eighth-grade student with a specific learning disability who is at risk due to her use of drugs and alcohol in her home. Which of the following initial interventions would likely be most beneficial in helping Courtney focus on school?

a. Offering to meet with her and her parents
b. Offering to take her to rehabilitation
c. Offering to refer her to a counselor
d. Offering to keep her secret safe

69. Martin is a 12th-grade student with an intellectual disability who is learning to do his own laundry at school. Which one of the following examples includes maintenance and generalization when working on this skill?

a. Practicing doing laundry every day at school
b. Practicing doing laundry once a week at school
c. Practicing doing laundry every day at the laundromat
d. Practicing doing laundry once a week at the laundromat

70. Which one of the following instructional strategies allows students to move around the room while still learning?

a. Embodied learning
b. Inquiry-based learning
c. Blended learning
d. Service learning

71. Patrick is a third-grade student with IEP goals in math problem-solving and math calculations. What is the best instructional strategy to provide a spiraling curriculum?

a. Reviewing class material using similar instructional methods
b. Completing upcoming homework assignments in advance
c. Implementing both visual and auditory explanations of math content he learns in school
d. Increasing the complexity of the math work and problems gradually as he gains mastery

72. When working with a general education math teacher, which instructional strategy would be the best in allowing a student with a visual impairment access to the curriculum?

a. Modified assignment length
b. An audio version of the textbook
c. Preferential seating close to the board
d. Extended time on tests

73. Which of the following is NOT an accurate statement regarding teaching reading skills to students with learning disabilities?

a. Using both visual and auditory input greatly increases comprehension.
b. Using both visual and auditory input greatly increases reading speed.
c. Using both visual and auditory input distracts and confuses students.
d. Using both visual and auditory input works better than either alone.

74. A middle school language arts teacher begins each class with 10 minutes of journal writing. Students are free to write about whatever they choose. She reminds them this is the perfect place to react to something they've read, write about a problem and try to think of solutions, track a project they've undertaken, and otherwise interact honestly with themselves. The teacher should periodically:

a. Collect the journals and select an entry to edit; this will show the students how their writing can improve.
b. Suggest new and innovative ways students can use their journals, including automatic writing, found poetry, lists, and collages.
c. Collect and review the journals to identify students at risk for drugs, alcohol, or sexual abuse.
d. Say nothing about the journals during the school year. They are intensely private and discussing them in any way with the students violates trust.

75. Keith has a behavior disorder and expressive language deficits. His teacher wants to evaluate his progress toward his IEP goals for behavior. Which of the following would be the most appropriate method?

a. Norm-referenced testing
b. Interviewing Keith
c. Observational assessment
d. Curriculum-based testing

76. A new high school student is being assessed. He reads a 500-word text. He misreads 35 words. At what level is he reading?

a. Instructional level
b. Independent level
c. Unsatisfactory level
d. Merit level

77. Which type of assessment compares a student's performance on a test to a national average for age/grade level?

a. Norm-referenced test
b. Criterion-referenced test
c. Performance-based test
d. Ipsative measure/test

78. Identifying specific skills deficient in special education math students is important so the teacher can decide how to remediate. Problems can include an inability to recall math facts, focus on details, or understand mathematical operations and formulas and how rules are used in solving problems. Such students might be:

a. Able to solve math problems when they haven't been taught an operation required to do so
b. Unable to locate errors in their own work
c. Able to solve math problems in another language
d. Unable to count higher than 100

79. What type of tests compare students with other students?

a. Norm-referenced tests
b. Criterion-referenced tests
c. Subject assessment tests
d. Performance-based tests

80. If you were assessing a deaf student who is completely nonverbal, which of these would NOT be appropriate for IQ testing purposes?

a. Leiter
b. Raven's Progressive Matrices
c. TONI-III
d. Stanford-Binet

81. Cara and Mia both took the same IQ test. Cara received a score of 119 on the test, which has a mean of 100 and a standard deviation of 15. Mia received a score of 125. Which of the following is true about these scores?

a. Mia is smarter than Cara because she scored higher.
b. Mia's score was above average and Cara's was average.
c. Cara and Mia both scored above average on this IQ test.
d. Cara and Mia both had average scores on this IQ test.

82. Which of the following is the best example of how to interpret the results of a diagnostic assessment?

a. To determine the instructional level that students are at
b. To determine the disability that a student may have
c. To determine the kind of special education services that a student needs
d. To determine the amount that a student has learned

83. When determining the continued eligibility for a student with a specific learning disability, which of the following tests would be most appropriate to administer?

a. Intelligence test
b. Achievement test
c. Screening test
d. Curriculum-based test

84. Which of the following strategies is most effective in measuring the goals of students with behavior concerns?

a. Using curriculum-based measures
b. Comparing students to their peers
c. Counting the number of referrals
d. Using random time samples

85. Sasha is a kindergarten student who seems to be struggling with the curriculum in her class. Which of the following screening tests would be LEAST likely to benefit Sasha before determining whether or not a special education evaluation is appropriate?

a. Communication screening
b. Hearing and vision screening
c. Motor skills screening
d. Cognitive screening

86. Which of the following is the best example of how a student with a specific learning disability can access standardized tests?

a. Allowing them to access alternate tests
b. Allowing them to access modified tests
c. Allowing them to access accommodated tests
d. Allowing them to access differentiated tests

87. Tristan is a 10th-grade student with a specific learning disability in the area of reading comprehension. Which of the following examples would likely be the most beneficial in administering summative assessments to students like Tristan?

a. Administering alternate assessments
b. Administering assessments with modifications
c. Administering assessments with accommodations
d. Administering informal assessments

88. Which of the following best describes alternate assessments and students that receive special education services?

a. Most students who receive special education services take alternate assessments.
b. Students who take alternate assessments do not receive high school diplomas.
c. Parents have the option to choose whether students take alternate assessments.
d. Alternate assessments must be based on grade-level standards.

89. Which of the following best describes the use of a screening test for struggling students?

a. To determine eligibility for special education services
b. To determine whether an in-depth assessment must be conducted
c. To determine a student's progress on IEP goals and objectives
d. To determine which classes a student should take

90. Joseph is a fourth-grade student being evaluated for special education services as a student with a specific learning disability in the area of math problem solving. Which of the following would be the best interpretation of his assessment results that show he is within one standard deviation of the mean in math problem solving?

a. Joseph would likely be determined eligible for special education services.
b. Joseph would likely need more testing in order to determine his eligibility.
c. Joseph would likely be determined ineligible for special education services.
d. Joseph would likely be determined eligible for a 504 Plan instead.

91. Which of the following is typically the most challenging when identifying whether an English learner qualifies for special education services?

a. It can be difficult to determine whether the student' s difficulties are due to lack of mastery of the language or a disability.
b. The Individualized Education Program (IEP) may not meet their needs.
c. Special education services may not be beneficial in English.
d. The student may already miss too much class.

92. How can the interpretation of curriculum-based assessments be valuable in determining the growth of a student?

a. By comparing the student's score to others in the district
b. By comparing the student's score to their grade in the class
c. By comparing the student's score to the average score
d. By comparing the student's score to their previous scores

93. Which of the following students would it be most appropriate to conduct a verbal intelligence test on when reevaluating for special education services?

a. A student with an intellectual disability
b. A student with a specific learning disability in math
c. A student with a specific learning disability in writing
d. A student with a visual impairment

94. When conducting an assessment in the area of fine motor skills, which of the following activities would be the most important to observe?

a. Watching a student draw a picture
b. Watching a student make numbers with their hands
c. Watching a student throw a ball
d. Watching a student ride a bike

95. What steps are taken to identify specific skill deficits in math?

a. Standardized assessment tests, examining areas of weakness in student work to determine patterns, teacher observations, interviews with the student.
b. Standardized assessment tests, examining areas of weakness in student work to determine patterns, teacher observations, interviews with parents.
c. Teacher observations coupled with examining areas of weakness in student work are sufficient.
d. None of the above

96. Which of the following is the goal of implementing a summative assessment?

a. To evaluate student learning
b. To determine the appropriate instruction
c. To monitor student learning
d. To compare students to a norm

97. What was the first major federal law guaranteeing all children aged 5–21 the right to a public education?

a. IDEA
b. EHA
c. FAPE
d. LRE

98. Which of the following strategies is likely to be most effective in overcoming any kind of personal cultural biases when working with students with disabilities?

a. Learning about why the cultural bias occurs
b. Being objective when evaluating these students
c. Treating each of the students the same way
d. Encouraging cross-group participation among peers

99. In an IEP meeting, who is the best choice to interpret a student's evaluation results?

a. Whoever can best explain the educational implications of those results
b. The student's special education teacher on the IEP team
c. The school psychologist, who may or may not be an IEP team member
d. Another professional who is not a part of the student's IEP team

100. Which of the following is an independent federal agency that makes recommendations to both the President and Congress regarding issues related to disabilities?

a. Federation for Children with Special Needs (FCSN)
b. Center for Personal Assistance Services (CPAS)
c. National Disability Rights Network (NDRN)
d. The National Council on Disability (NCD)

101. Before being assigned to a special education classroom, a student must:

a. Agree to the reassignment.
b. Have an Individualized Education Program developed.
c. Have a Section 504 plan developed.
d. Be seen by an educational psychologist to confirm diagnosis.

102. A fifth-grade lead teacher and the special education teacher have scheduled a parent conference to discuss the behavior problems of the student. They anticipate the boy's mother will be anxious and defensive like she has been at previous conferences. The best approach for the teachers to take is to:

a. Draw the parent out about issues in her own life so that she will feel reassured and trusting. Point out possible connections between the mother's emotions about her own life and her son's behaviors and reactions.
b. Be very firm with the mother, explain the penalties and disciplines her son can expect if the behavior continues, and stress that neither the parent nor the child has input regarding punishment.
c. Emphasize that the teachers will not do anything without the parent's approval since they do not want to face liability issues.
d. Begin by welcoming the mother and telling her about her son's academic improvements. Assure her that the teachers, the mother, and the child share goals for the student's success. Explain the behavior problems and ask if the mother has any insights to share.

103. The ADA is:

a. The Americans with Disabilities Act
b. The Anti-Discrimination Act
c. The American Diabetes Association
d. The Alternatives to Discrimination Act

104. Students with learning disabilities will typically spend part or all of their day in what type of classroom?

a. General classroom
b. Solitary classroom
c. Special education classroom
d. Language learning classroom

105. What legislation gives students and families increased protection in regard to the confidentiality of student records?

a. No Child Left Behind Act
b. Americans with Disabilities Act
c. Family Educational Rights and Privacy Act
d. Human Equity Act

106. Nina is a student who has severe hearing impairment. She wears a hearing aid and has a low level of hearing. She can communicate verbally but speaks very loudly. Nina visited the public library in the past, but the local librarian was upset at the disruption created by her loud speech. The librarian now does not like Nina and does not want her in the library. What does Nina's special education teacher do?

a. She tells Nina that the school library is just as good and that she should do all her library activities at school instead of aggravating the local librarian and putting up with her rejection.
b. She supervises Nina during visits to the public library and teaches her to control her voice while there; she also helps establish a friendly relationship between Nina and the librarian.
c. She complains to the school principal about the local librarian, saying she is discriminating against Nina because of her disability.
d. She sends Nina to the school psychologist for counseling to console her after her feelings have been hurt by the local librarian's disapproval.

107. Tina is a student with a seizure disorder. Despite medication, she has sustained head injuries during past seizures. She now wears a helmet to protect her against further injuries. Other students, general education teachers, and various people in the community do not know why she wears the helmet and have a lot of misconceptions about it. How can her special education teacher help?

a. Recommend that Tina not wear the helmet in public anymore because it is too stigmatizing.
b. Recommend that Tina not wear the helmet in public and have someone accompany her at all times to prevent head injuries if she has a seizure.
c. Educate general education teachers and other school and community personnel about the helmet and enlist their aid to educate others about it.
d. Advise Tina that it is her sole responsibility to explain to everybody she encounters daily about her helmet and about why she needs to wear it.

108. Carly is an elementary school student who uses a wheelchair. Two small plastic parts on her chair have broken, rendering it unusable. Carly is using an uncomfortable "loaner" chair. She is unhappy without her own chair. Carly's parents are having financial difficulties. Carly's teacher sees these things and wants to do something. Which of the following might she do?

a. She finds a charitable group that repairs wheelchairs for free.
b. She does nothing, because this is not her job as a teacher.
c. She pays for the repair herself to help Carly's parents.
d. She finds a charity to donate a new chair to Carly.

109. Which of the following best describes how often at minimum a behavior intervention plan should be updated?

a. Once a year at the annual IEP meeting
b. Each time the student has a new teacher
c. On every progress report date
d. As the IEP team deems it necessary

110. Which of the following is true about discipline and students who receive special education services according to IDEA?

a. Manifestation determinations are required for students with disabilities when they are subjected to a disciplinary change of placement.
b. Students with disabilities cannot be suspended more than 10 days.
c. Discipline for special education students is the same as general education.
d. Special education services are not provided for expelled students.

111. Which of the following agencies would likely best help high school students with specific learning disabilities find and maintain jobs?

a. School-to-work agencies
b. Independent living agencies
c. College counseling agencies
d. Military recruiting agencies

112. Marie is a fifth-grade student who receives special education services as a student with a hearing impairment. Which of the following sections in the IEP describes the support that Marie will receive specific to her disability?

a. Communication plan
b. Annual goals
c. Accommodations
d. Special factors

113. Which of the following is NOT one of the components of a free appropriate public education (FAPE)?

a. All children with disabilities are entitled to FAPE.
b. Schools must provide the best possible education.
c. Schools must notify parents of proposals to change their child's placement.
d. Special education and related services must be provided at public expense.

114. Which one of the following challenges is LEAST likely to arise when collaborating with parents at IEP meetings?

a. Differences with regard to IEP goals
b. Differences with regard to accommodations
c. Differences with regard to attendance issues
d. Differences with regard to service delivery

115. Jose is a fourth-grade student who was recently determined to be eligible for special education services. Which of the following strategies would be most beneficial in supporting his family?

a. Providing them with fact sheets about his disability
b. Holding informational meetings regularly
c. Allowing them to shadow his classes
d. Giving them a list of outside providers

116. Which of the following best describes how students who receive special education services are also protected under Section 504 of the Rehabilitation Act of 1973?

a. Students who receive special education services also receive 504 Plans.
b. Students who exit special education must receive 504 Plans.
c. Students with 504 Plans also receive special education services.
d. Students who received special education services prior to graduating high school can qualify for 504 Plans in college.

117. Which of the following best describes the purpose of the prior written notice section of the IEP?

a. To invite parents to the IEP meeting
b. To provide copies of rights to parents
c. To propose changes to the IEP
d. To end special education services

118. Which of the following would LEAST likely be one of the responsibilities of the school psychologist with regard to providing support for students with disabilities?

a. Providing mental health support
b. Administering IQ tests to students
c. Training staff on behavior plan implementation
d. Providing special education instruction

119. Which of the following is true of the Family Educational Rights and Privacy Act with regard to students who receive special education services?

a. These protections also apply to private schools.
b. The school cannot release records without parental consent.
c. Parents do not have the right to request educational records.
d. Parental rights belong to the student when they turn 18.

120. Which of the following strategies would be LEAST effective in communicating to parents as the new case manager of a student?

a. Calling them with an introduction
b. Setting up a meeting to discuss the IEP
c. Sending home a note for the student to deliver
d. Meeting them in person when they pick up their child

Answer Key and Explanations for Test #1

1. A: With students who have disabilities, the time to introduce each career development stage depends more on the individual student's developmental level, which often is not commensurate with the student's grade level (B) or chronological age (D) in some or all domains. While the student's experiential level (C) is important for selecting instructional materials and methods, the developmental level has more impact on whether a student will be able to learn the skills acquired in each stage.

2. C: The most likely diagnosis is autism. Autistic children are typically very withdrawn, avoid eye contact, and are not responsive to verbal or physical attempts to connect. Some autistic children fall into repetitive behaviors that are very difficult to arrest or prevent. These behaviors include rocking, spinning and hand shaking.

3. A: Counting money, planning meals, grocery shopping, recognizing safety concerns. These are among the most basic life skills students with developmental delays must master. Other life skills include specific occupational skills, home maintenance, clothes selection and care, food preparation, and personal hygiene.

4. A: Trip-training was successful in the previous, more restrictive setting. Even in the case of a less restrictive community setting, something that worked before will work again. The stress of the change and the decrease in structure probably contributed to the reemergence of Andrea's enuresis. Reapplying a technique familiar to her will remedy it. With her prior training, she will soon be getting up and going to the bathroom every two hours on her own. Therefore, option A is correct.

Trying to find a different strategy is unnecessary. This would only be indicated if trip-training had never been successful. Also, trip-training is not too restrictive a strategy for the group home. It is a technique that works well in any setting. Therefore, option B is incorrect.

Wearing adult diapers would be a step backward for Andrea. It is more restrictive and makes her less independent. It does not teach, remind, or encourage her to use constructive methods for bladder management. Therefore, option C is incorrect.

Wearing absorbent underwear seems more grown-up than diapers, but this still does not make use of Andrea's capacity to use techniques for bladder management, whereas trip-training does. Therefore, option D is incorrect.

5. A: The field of education is constantly changing; the same is true of policies and regulations pertaining to children with special needs. Teachers are usually the first people to identify or intervene when a child is struggling in class. All teachers should be responsible for educating themselves regarding possible problems that children might face. Without knowledge of symptoms, it will be impossible for a teacher to guide the student or parents effectively. The teacher may also find that previous knowledge of typical classroom strategies may benefit the child in question more quickly and may prevent problems from getting worse.

6. D: The child most likely has dyscalculia. Dyscalculia defines a range of difficulties in math, such as the inability to understand numbers' meanings, measurements, patterns, mathematical terms, and the application of mathematic principles. Early clues include a young child's inability to group items by size or color, recognize patterns, or understand the meaning or order of numbers.

7. D: Verbal dyspraxia is a motor skill development disorder which includes speech errors that don't clearly follow a pattern and so appear to be inconsistent. An example is a student who can pronounce /p/ when it is followed by a long i, as in pine, but not when followed by an ou diphthong, as in pout. Verbally dyspraxic individuals are unable to correctly place the tongue, lips and jaw for consistent sounds that can be organized into syllables. Dyspraxia appears to be a brain disorder in which the area that controls production of particular sounds is damaged.

8. A: An eight-year-old child with profound intellectual disabilities is at a developmental level similar to that of a baby or toddler. As such, he is very busy exploring and learning about his environment by roaming around and interacting with it. Chewing on countertops reflects a baby's tendency to explore objects orally. Piaget would describe this as assimilating other activities into the child's early sucking schema established during nursing. Individuals whose cognitive development has only reached the level of a baby but whose physical development is farther along, and who thus have teeth, often have different results from mouthing objects than do toothless infants or toddlers with few teeth. Developmental level is the most likely reason for Christopher's behavior, so option A is correct.

There is no reason to assume Christopher lacks training. An eight-year-old with a profound level of intellectual disabilities could be receiving excellent training, but considering his level of disability, progress may nevertheless be very slow. Christopher's energy level is high, as evidenced by his activity level. A particular training program might modify his behavior, but it cannot be assumed that what he does is a result of a lack of training. His behaviors are developmentally typical of a younger child, congruent with his cognitive level, so option B is incorrect.

This child has multiple disabilities, but an impulse control disorder is not one of them. At the chronological age of eight years, it is quite normal for a boy to be physically very active. At Christopher's much lower cognitive age, it is normal to explore his environment and to mouth objects. Also, his behaviors do not include any specific symptoms of an impulse control disorder such as screaming, grabbing, hitting, uncontrolled eating/drinking, or other behaviors that could indicate this disorder in a child of his chronological and mental ages, so option C is incorrect.

No information is given about the school environment here. While it is possible Christopher is searching for additional stimulation, it is equally possible that this school is a stimulus-rich environment that motivates him to move around and explore the various stimuli. His high activity level would not necessarily accompany boredom or lack of stimulation. With no information about the environment, it is impossible to assume he does not find it stimulating enough, so option D is incorrect.

9. D: Although students with autism spectrum disorder may suffer from orthopedic impairments at a higher rate than their peers, this is not typically one of the co-occurring conditions. Students with autism tend to suffer from many mental and physical conditions. According to Autism Speaks, the largest autism advocacy organization in the United States, many of these conditions co-occur with students diagnosed with autism. Answer A is incorrect because anxiety is common with students with autism. Answer B is incorrect because epilepsy is also a commonly co-occurring condition with autistic students. Answer C is incorrect because sleep conditions are also very common.

10. D: Charles is not described as having conflicts with other residents or caregivers. While he might not like people in his new placement, such information is not provided. Therefore, option A is incorrect.

Someone can be expected to do less well initially with less structure after doing well with more structure. But staying indefinitely in the same program would constitute a lack of progress. To satisfy goals of normalization and inclusion in the least restrictive setting, the trend is to move from residential facilities to community settings. With Charles' success in the more restrictive environment, progressing to the community would be a goal for him. There is no reason to assume the skills he has learned cannot be transferred to the community or that he will always need a more restrictive setting. He did regress to his former behaviors under the stress of change, but this was not inevitable. Given his favorable response to the training he received, regression could have been avoided. Therefore, option B is incorrect.

Charles may have been used to the residential campus, making the group home seem uncomfortably foreign to him. But if that were the only reason for his unhappiness, he might be expected to return to the residential facility when running away, rather than going downtown and having no place to live. Therefore, option C is incorrect.

Change is uncomfortable, especially for someone used to a very structured routine. Moving to a group home might make Charles feel insecure and threaten his stability. To accomplish such a move, careful preparation and planning is needed by current and future caregivers to ensure an effective transition between the two settings. Charles would need ongoing counseling, including before, during, and after the move. Advance meetings with new housemates and staff are also necessary. Ensuring Charles' continued contact with friends and staff from the former facility is advisable. Some shared social and work activities that include people from both settings could be helpful. It would be important for counselors to know Charles' feelings about the move and to help him address any anxieties or objections he has. Running away indicates not just regression but a lack of communication with him about his new placement. Therefore, option D is correct.

11. A: Learning to prepare simple meals in the kitchen of a home-like building on campus with a teacher's guidance is a good exercise for Dick. It will prepare him further for community living since he has never previously learned to prepare meals. Learning to do so will make him more independent in the community and increase the number of settings in which he can live successfully. Therefore option A is correct.

In Dick's current situation as an individual with mild intellectual disabilities, practical daily living skills such as meal preparation are a higher priority than adding more general academic subjects, because he already has basic work and self-care skills but has never learned to cook. Therefore option B is incorrect.

Practicing hardware sorting is not necessary for Dick as he has already learned to do simple jobs like this in the campus workshop. Therefore option C is incorrect.

Practicing personal care and dressing is not necessary since Dick has already learned these skills and performs them well. Therefore option D is incorrect.

12. C: In the third statement, Mr. Shirley is encouraging Billy by first showing his belief and confidence in Billy's ability and then conveying his high expectations of Billy as well as his trust in him. Such a statement is likely to increase Billy's confidence and motivation to try his best, so option C is correct.

Offering sympathy is nice, but in option A, Mr. Shirley is coddling Billy. With his already low self-confidence, this statement is unlikely to motivate Billy to try harder or do better. Mr. Shirley has, in effect, given Billy permission to accept his current level of performance and not to improve, so option A is incorrect.

Option B is negative in character. High teacher expectations can increase student motivation but only if they are positive in nature. This statement is critical and will only reinforce Billy's feelings of inadequacy, so option B is incorrect.

In option D, Mr. Shirley is just excusing Billy from trying. He is, in effect, inviting Billy to give up if something seems too difficult. This kind of statement would feed into Billy's low self-confidence and confirm his insecurities that he cannot succeed, so he may as well not bother to try; therefore, option D is incorrect.

13. A: Many communities have community-based supported employment agencies that help individuals with intellectual disabilities secure jobs. These agencies, such as TASH (The Association for Persons with Severe Handicaps), provide resources for transition from school to adult life, help match individuals to jobs they can do, and offer ongoing support. Of all the options, contacting a local community-based supported employment agency (A) would be most helpful for Debbie to find a job she could realistically do and be hired for. Option B is incorrect because simply searching want ads is unlikely to result in a job Debbie can perform or be hired for and would probably waste the teacher's time. Option C is incorrect because teaching Debbie to search want ads might build a skill, but it is unlikely to help her find a suitable job and could lead to frustration or disappointment. Option D is incorrect because having her parents apply for jobs on her behalf does not involve Debbie in the process, teaches her nothing, and is unlikely to result in successful employment.

14. B: Because these students are all English language learners (ELLs), it is more likely that this is the true source of their reading difficulties rather than learning disabilities. Therefore, option B is correct.

The only way to identify a true learning disability with reading would be to test these students in reading both English and their native language. It is impossible to assume they all have learning disabilities regardless of language without ruling out the impact of their ELL status. Therefore, option A is incorrect.

Since English is a second language for these students, it cannot be assumed that the first or most likely cause of their reading difficulties is a learning disability. Therefore, option C is incorrect.

It is so common for ELLs to perform less well in reading English than native English speakers that it is highly unlikely for reading problems and ELL status to be a complete coincidence with every student in the group. Therefore, option D is incorrect.

15. C: Although some of these choices may be true in certain situations, parents of students with disabilities will typically see some of the signs before the child is evaluated at school. The parents likely spend a good deal of time with these children, so they are aware of what they can and can't do. They may not know for certain whether or not a student has a disability, but they can determine what they struggle with at home. Answer A is incorrect because families of children with disabilities are more likely to experience issues than they are to come together. Answer B is incorrect because parents are not the cause of the learning disability and also cannot be the cure. Answer D is incorrect because while some families do often seek out information to learn more about disabilities, this is not as consistently seen as families suspecting a disability is present in a child before the school does.

16. C: A typical four-year-old would be expected to start cutting paper with scissors. This is an example of a fine motor skill because it is a skill that uses small muscles such as those of the hands and fingers rather than large muscles. It is important to recognize the difference between fine and gross motor skills in order to determine which may be age appropriate or could potentially be a deficit. Answer A is incorrect because hopping on one foot uses larger muscles groups so it would be an example of gross motor skills. Answer B is incorrect because catching a ball also would be considered an example of gross motor skills. Answer D is incorrect because riding a tricycle also involves the larger muscle groups in the legs.

17. C: Although students in each disability category will often access these community services, students with multiple disabilities tend to be impacted the most and have the highest chance of using community services. The community services section of the transition goals includes services that will need to be in place for students who struggle to live on their own. Students with multiple disabilities are often impacted to the point that they will have a difficult time living independently and can benefit from services through the community. Answer A is incorrect because although some students with autism spectrum disorder will access community services, this is not always the case. Answer B is incorrect because students with emotional disturbances are impacted in a wide variety of ways and many times, these students do not access community services. Answer D is incorrect because students with traumatic brain injuries are also impacted in many ways, many of which do not result in accessing community services.

18. B: Children with congenital rubella, or who are exposed in utero to maternal rubella, are NOT more likely to suffer paralysis. Rubella (German measles) causes birth defects related to the sensory systems of vision and hearing. Babies exposed to rubella are more likely to suffer from deafness (A), blindness (C), and/or cataracts (D) of the eyes, which interfere with normal vision.

19. C: Although all of these choices can be effective in helping a student achieve their ultimate goal, the postsecondary transition goal is simply what the student is seeking to achieve. Although the goal does have to be realistic and something that the student is interested in, the goal may or may not be met in the future. Postsecondary transition goals in the area of employment are important in guiding the students toward careers that they may have an interest in pursuing. While Answer A may be a training step Jimmy needs to take, it is incorrect because going to college is an example of an education goal, and the goal does not include Jimmy becoming an actual veterinarian. Answer B is incorrect because researching the job requirements is more of listing the steps the student will take to reach the goal. Answer D is incorrect because this is more about what will help him reach his ultimate goal.

20. A: Although reaching out to colleges in the area may or may not result in responses from those schools, they are most likely to respond if they hear from Gordon. It is important for Gordon to feel empowered to reach out to these schools on his own in order to develop independence. Involving Gordon in the process allows him to feel like he owns the experience and is making his own path for the future. Answer B is incorrect because assisting Gordon in researching colleges can help him narrow his choices. Answer C is incorrect because helping him find jobs he may want will allow him to find out what schools offer certain programs. Answer D is incorrect because allowing him to practice application writing will help him with the actual application procedure.

21. D: Carefully planning what the content of the math instruction covers and the order in which it is taught (A), using their best judgment in choosing and applying appropriate teaching strategies (B), and designing practice activities with a wide range of student needs in mind (C) are all actions by teachers that will improve the involvement and progress of all students, including those with special needs. The action most likely to be needed specifically by some special needs students in the general education classroom is using more intensive direct instruction methods to teach them basic mathematics.

22. B: Modern society demands greater literacy today than in the past. For example, as cited by Dr. Rebecca C. Faulkner, the Air Force manual for repairing fighter planes was seven pages long in World War II and 7,000 pages long in 2008. The same literacy skills in students do not apply across all subjects (A) because different literacy skills are needed for different content areas. Literacy required of school pupils also does not stay constant across grades (C) because literacy requirements advance along with each advance in grade level. Finally, literacy is not best taught in schools as a separate lesson (D) because that would be insufficient; in order to meet the changing demands of society, literacy must be taught and incorporated throughout the school day.

23. D: Students with attention-deficit/hyperactivity disorder are generally extremely sensitive to distractions. A learning environment in which visual and audio distractions have been eliminated is best. Low lighting, few posters, and a clean whiteboard will help minimize distractions.

24. D: Memorize their lists by using techniques such as songs, mnemonic devices, and other fun activities. By definition, irregular sight words cannot be decoded but must be recognized on sight.

25. C: The physical environment of a classroom is very important to effective learning. Classrooms that are bare will promote a cold, institutional feeling. This may inhibit learning. On the other hand, classrooms cluttered with information and posters may be too overwhelming for students and thus be counterproductive. In addition to ensuring that posters with appropriate content and an appropriate amount of information are used to decorate a room, proper lighting is also essential for creating an effective learning environment. Adequate lighting should be used to maintain attention and to prevent a dark environment where students and the teacher become sleepy during the day. This is especially important after lunch. If a classroom does not have enough lighting, the teacher can use lamps to increase the brightness of a room.

26. C: The teacher is making appropriate modifications. Each child is different. In this case, she has consulted with the special education teacher and concluded the child needs multiple supports.

27. B: While setting rules and establishing routines is important to classroom management, the teacher should not be so firm that there is no room for flexibility and adjustments. A teacher's relationship with a child must remain consistent in terms of the teacher's interactions with the child and the expectations set for the child; a moody or fickle teacher can frustrate and anger the children. Teachers should respond to children positively and avoid negativity for the relationship to be constructive and nurturing. Although the teacher is the ultimate decision-maker in the classroom and must establish authority, sharing power with the children by guiding them into making responsible choices gives the children a sense of empowerment and a stake in the classroom situation.

28. D: Peer helpers are more likely to keep the restless student on task than to distract that student; therefore, peer helpers are a good idea. Allowing a student who has trouble staying on task to do a "gallery walk"; that is, to expend some energy by walking around to examine the lesson materials that are on display, is a good practice because once the student has seen the materials he or she is less likely to be distracted by wondering about them. A student who has trouble staying on task is helped by being assigned specific tasks to accomplish because breaking up the assignment into smaller jobs seems more achievable. Using response cards catches the attention of the student who has trouble staying on task and pulls that student into the lesson with the others.

29. A: Teachers will not always know a student's preferred communication mode. For example, deaf students often use sign language rather than speech. This is also true of learning modalities, such as blind students reading in Braille. Many teachers do not know either of these systems but must be able to provide adaptations to meet these students' special needs. They can procure Braille texts without learning Braille, and they can obtain live, online, or video sign language interpreters without learning sign language. Teachers may also need to differentiate instruction based on gender, because learning is not always the same for boys as it is for girls (B). Teachers are likely, especially with disability and diversity populations, to encounter age differences in one class (C). Learning English is not the sole responsibility of students (D) because many English Language Learner programs and methods are available to teachers.

30. B: Derrick can only use one arm and hand, so assembly of small machine parts would be difficult and frustrating. Therefore, option A is incorrect.

Sorting small machine parts is more appropriate. Derrick's eyesight is good, so he can identify differences in shapes. He can pick up and place parts in separate containers with one hand. Therefore, option B is correct.

Assembly line work could involve standing up, but Derrick is in a wheelchair. It would also likely involve using both arms and hands, and it would probably require physical stamina and movement beyond Derrick's capabilities. Therefore, option C is incorrect.

Requisitioning and ordering parts would involve reading and writing. With profound intellectual disabilities, Derrick would be unable to do these things. In addition to filling out forms, this job could also involve speaking, which Derrick cannot do. Therefore, option D is incorrect.

31. A: The paraprofessional can assist with physical needs. The aide can check Clarence's work but should refer re-teaching and assignment of exercises to Mr. Hunt. The parent volunteer is a good choice to give Misty emotional support. Daisy and Carmela are the best choices for peer tutoring since they are very alike in age and grade level but are opposites when it comes to strengths and weaknesses in math and reading. Therefore, option A is correct.

The paraprofessional can check Clarence's work but should not explain or assign exercises. The teacher should do these things. The parent volunteer may or may not be comfortable taking children other than her own to the bathroom. Misty may appreciate the peer approval implicit in receiving emotional support from Daisy and Carmela, but she may also prefer adult approval. Since Daisy and Carmela's strengths and weaknesses are so opposite and their other characteristics are so similar, their helping each other is a more directly beneficial use of peer tutoring. If both girls are busy supporting Misty, they will have less time and attention to help each other and make their own progress. Although the teacher can give physical help with arts and crafts when he is the only adult in the class, since others are present who can help with this, he can do more teaching. Therefore, option B is incorrect.

As the teacher, Mr. Hunt should not be taking students to the bathroom while the volunteer, the paraprofessional, and the aide do his teaching tasks. Therefore, option C is incorrect.

In option D, Mr. Hunt is doing too many things considering how many helpers he has in his room. He is supporting Misty, helping the physically disabled students with arts and crafts, and also taking them to the bathroom. At the same time, the paraprofessional and the volunteer are doing his teaching tasks. Therefore, option D is incorrect.

32. C: Proactive strategies are used to prevent the escalation of behavior. If the behavior is already escalating, it is too late to apply such strategies, so option A is incorrect.

Reinforcement of any behavior strengthens the likelihood that the behavior will recur. The worst possible time to present reinforcement would be during the escalation of a tantrum. Doing so would increase the escalation and increase the odds of additional future tantrums; therefore, option B is incorrect.

Proactive strategies would be aimed at preventing the tantrum from escalating. These could redirect Annie's behavior and/or differentially reinforce other behavior, so option C is correct.

Tension reduction is the phase at the end of a tantrum, once the aggression, self-injury, and/or destruction are over. Typically, Annie would be crying, exhausted, and contrite at this stage. This would be far too late for proactive strategies. This would be a better time for support and debriefing; therefore, option D is incorrect.

33. C: Verbal de-escalation is a way of reducing tension early in the behavior—before it becomes violent—without resorting to physical means. This would be most appropriate given the information on Bruce's behavior. Therefore, option C is correct.

Bruce responds well to de-escalation and rarely becomes violent with early intervention. Physical restraint would thus be an entirely inappropriate form of early intervention. Therefore, option A is incorrect.

Mechanical restraint is even more restrictive than physical restraint. Since Bruce responds well to de-escalation techniques, mechanical (or any) restraint is not indicated as an early intervention. Therefore, option B is incorrect.

Bruce's behavior assessment shows that his behavior is not attention-seeking. Extinction, or planned ignoring, addresses behaviors that seek attention. Without attention, such behaviors eventually stop, as they are not producing the desired effect. Behaviors that indicate attention seeking do not necessarily stop if the individual is ignored. If it is not de-escalated, Bruce's behavior may become violent. Extinction would be both ineffective and dangerous in his case. Therefore, option D is incorrect.

34. B: Regional and magnet schools for deaf students currently only exist in a few locations in the country, so students often have to live away from home to attend them. This would not be an example of inclusive education. Therefore, option B is correct.

Attending general education schools and being pulled out for special education instruction is one inclusive solution for deaf students. Therefore, option A is incorrect.

Teaching sign language to all students and teachers in the general education setting is another inclusive strategy. Therefore, option C is incorrect.

Assigning interpreters to the classrooms for deaf students who use sign language is another inclusive strategy. Therefore, option D is incorrect.

35. C: Although all these arrangements may have their benefits for certain students, clusters easily allow students and teachers to work together and move from group to group. Active teaching and learning enable the students to move around and work with different students. This cluster arrangement allows this movement for all students, including those with disabilities who may need to be accessed quickly and easily. Answer A is incorrect because traditional rows and columns tend to be more teacher-centered and do not allow for much movement throughout the room. Answer B is incorrect because although the horseshoe shape can provide space for the teacher to move, it doesn't provide as much freedom for the students. Answer D is incorrect because runway seating tends to be beneficial for teacher movement, but the students wouldn't be able to move as much.

36. D: Maintenance is important in ensuring that students are able to retain the information that they have learned on a particular topic. In order to do this, the students must practice the skill regularly to ensure that it is not forgotten. Depending on the skill, this may mean daily, weekly, or monthly practice in order to maintain what has already been learned. Answer A is incorrect because performing the skill in a variety of settings would be an example of generalization. Answer B is incorrect because simply practicing the skill when it is learned may make it difficult to maintain the skill. Answer C is incorrect because progressing on the skill can be helpful, but this may not necessarily help in maintaining the learned skill.

37. C: Although all these choices can help in making sure the classroom is a safe environment, reporting student behavior to the parents immediately can be most effective. When students misbehave, this must be communicated to the parents so further action can potentially be taken. If it is not reported to parents, students may continue with these poor behaviors and put other students at risk. Answer A is incorrect because simply sending home the class rules may not work for every parent, and they may not always keep track of them. Answer B is incorrect because although getting to know the background of the parents might be helpful, this may not benefit the safety of the class. Answer D is incorrect because only reporting the positive behavior can help to build a safe classroom, but it is more important to report negative behavior that might be a safety concern.

38. B: Although it may be easier in some aspects to have all of the students that need additional support together, this might create some issues. It is important to strategically place these students based on their needs and behavior. The teacher must be able to access these students in different ways that promote a safe and supportive classroom. Answer A is incorrect because randomly placing them could potentially create issues with their peers. Answer C is incorrect because if they are clustered together, they may feel singled out for being different from the other students. Answer D is incorrect because just putting them at the front could also isolate them.

39. B: Supplementary curriculum is typically designed to provide opportunities for students to explore experiences that they might be interested in after high school. This may look different for each student, but it can be beneficial in providing students opportunities that they may not otherwise have. A supplementary curriculum can be used for all students but is typically designed for students who may need additional support in accessing a job after high school. Answer A is incorrect because supplementary curriculum typically does not simply mean that the students can access their accommodations. Answer C is incorrect because although assistive technology can be involved in supplementary curriculum, it may not always be. Answer D is incorrect because a supplementary curriculum is not meant to create more work for the students.

40. D: Although it may be possible to increase friendships when implementing a social skills group, this is not likely to be the goal of the intervention. Social skills interventions may be appropriate for students who struggle socially for many reasons, including exhibiting poor social skills and behavioral struggles. It may not necessarily be appropriate to implement a social skills group simply to provide an opportunity for a student to make friends. Answer A is incorrect because teaching social problem-solving skills can be an effective way to build social skills. Answer B is incorrect because teaching appropriate behavior can be helpful for students who struggle to exhibit reasonable behavior. Answer C is incorrect because decreasing antisocial behaviors can be beneficial to students who struggle to communicate with others.

41. D: The love and logic behavior management model would likely be most effective for a student like Jessie because he likely needs positive attention and reinforcement. The love and logic method allows the student and teacher to have a conversation and work through some of the solutions using loving ways. Students with emotional disturbances sometimes struggle with consequences and following strict rules and regulations. Answer A is incorrect because assertive discipline states that students must follow specific rules, which may be difficult for a student with an emotional disturbance. Answer B is incorrect because the logical consequences model may give negative consequences that these students may struggle to react appropriately to. Answer C is incorrect because reality therapy requires that students manage their own behavior, and the question stem states that Jessie has difficulties with self-reflection.

42. A: Adaptive skills are skills that people use every day in order to function at home, school, or work. There are many skills in caring for oneself and accessing the community that are important to practice and complete in order to demonstrate understanding. When teaching these skills, it is important to provide opportunities to practice these tasks to determine what students have mastered and what skills need additional work. Answer B is incorrect because although improving reading ability is important, it would not likely help students in learning everyday skills to function. It is more of an academic skill. Answer C is incorrect because learning about organization is not typically a skill that is practiced in isolation when considering adaptive skills. Answer D is incorrect because although basic math skills are also important skills, they would not be the most effective skill to teach when working on a student's adaptive skills.

43. C: Engaging with a student through argument, negotiation, or appeal may prove to be the least effective strategy because it will likely make the behavior escalate. Many students are simply trying to get attention, and if they are given the attention they seek, they are going to make matters worse. Furthermore, it is inappropriate to negotiate or engage with a student openly in a class with other students because it could embarrass the student or perhaps even make it seem like they are getting special privledge over the other students. It would be a better option to remain calm and possibly seek some assistance if needed. Answer A is incorrect because ignoring her behavior may cause her to stop eventually, since she is not getting what she wants. Answer B is incorrect because calling for backup can be a great strategy, especially if there are safety concerns. Answer D is incorrect because removing her from class also might be the best option if the other students are being disturbed.

44. D: Out of the options given, modifying the content can help the most with her reading comprehension struggles. Modifying the content to include less reading or fewer questions she has to answer still allows her to learn most, if not all, of what her peers learn. It is important to understand how to provide support in a way that students can still learn what their general education peers are learning whenever possible. Answer A is incorrect because it may alienate Anna to move her down a grade level. Answer B is incorrect because although reteaching concepts may be beneficial, her time with the special education teacher may be better spent working on her reading comprehension abilities. Answer C is incorrect because providing support from a paraprofessional likely would not be as beneficial as modifying the curriculum.

45. C: Because students learn in different ways, it is important to incorporate differentiated instruction in order to create the best learning environment for all students. This involves providing choice and changing content, product, process, or environment based on student needs. Choice C gives students the option to choose a project format that works best for them, so it is an example of differentiated instruction. Options A and B are undifferentiated, as they provide the same content in the same way to all students. While choice D could be beneficial in expressing diversity and connecting with students of various nationalities, it also provides the same content in the same manner to all students.

46. A: Although it is typically thought of as a good teaching practice to incorporate different kinds of activities in a lesson, some students struggle with this change. Students with autism or ADHD may have a harder time adjusting to their daily routine being adjusted. Incorporating some elements of the same activity every day might be best for some students' needs. Answer B is incorrect because even if students do not all have the knowledge that is required, the activity might be designed to give them that knowledge. Answer C is incorrect because it is best practice to monitor which students can work together and which students cannot. Answer D is incorrect because though it is important to implement the activities a student can complete according to their IEP, a variety of activities should still be offered so that each student can still feel included in the class.

47. A: Although functional curriculum can be implemented for students of any age or disability, it is most often taught to students with intellectual disabilities. Functional curriculum focuses on life skills and other daily living skills that students will need after high school. It may be appropriate for certain students to start working on some of these skills as early as the elementary school level. Answer B is incorrect because students with specific learning disabilities likely would not access this curriculum until high school. Answer C is incorrect because students with speech or language impairments are not likely to need this curriculum to supplement their knowledge. Answer D is incorrect because students with developmental delays may or may not access this curriculum later on, but the elementary school age tends to be early for most students.

48. B: Manipulatives make the abstract concepts of mathematics more concrete for students, making them good choices for students whose levels of cognitive development allow more concrete than abstract thought. Historically they have been physical objects, but, this is no longer necessary with computer technology (A). Virtual manipulatives are available and are also found effective (C). For example, the University of Utah has developed (and continues to develop) the National Library of Virtual Manipulatives through a grant from the National Science Foundation. While students cannot handle virtual manipulatives like physical ones, they can still view and manipulate objects onscreen to see concept relationships and applications more concretely. These virtual programs are interactive and promote students' active engagement more than traditional math lessons typically do (D).

49. C: Initial phoneme identification is generally the first skill that is introduced. This involves identifying the sound at the beginning of a word. Phoneme blending is taking individual phonemes and combining them into a word, like blending /s/, /u/, and /n/ to make "sun." Phoneme segmenting (B) is the reverse of blending, or being able to identify the individual phonemes in a given word. In this case, given the word "sun," the student can break it down into /s/, /u/, and /n/. Students are also taught segmentation of initial, middle, and final phonemes. Phoneme substitution (D) involves the student's substituting one phoneme of a word to make another word. For example, with initial phonemes, given "cat," the student can make "sat," "mat," "hat," "bat," etc.

50. B: Asking students to create a play about the story as the teacher reads aloud would be the most effective strategy. This activity grounds the students in the story action as it is occurring. Acting it out ensures understanding; otherwise, the students will most likely stop the teacher and ask for clarification. Furthermore, by acting it out, students are incorporating understanding physically. They will be more likely to retain the story and be able to comprehend the meanings incorporated in it.

51. A: Letter-sound correspondence is the relationship between a spoken sound and the letters predictably used in English to transcribe them.

52. B: When done properly, grouping students can be beneficial. Teachers can create a heterogeneous group, mixing high and low achievers in the same work group, which will allow low achievers to learn from high achievers. Grouping all low achievers in one group typically does not result in a significant increase in academic performance. Conversely, grouping all high achievers together has been shown to result in increases in academic performance. Teachers should carefully assess the abilities of their students prior to creating groups. Additionally, teachers should regularly assess work groups to ensure that students are meeting expectations and to address issues or concerns that arise after the groups are created.

53. B: It helps students to stick to a task if the task is made more fun by adding novelty to it through games or personal interest materials. For students who have difficulty staying with and completing routine tasks, the teacher can employ certain strategies that will encourage the child to stick with the work. One way is to explain to the students about the importance of remaining on-task and monitoring oneself. Another way is to eliminate any part of the routine that really isn't necessary, such as copying sentences. Still another way is to break up the task into smaller time commitments. In this way, the student doesn't get too bored before being allowed to go to something else, but they are nonetheless required to come back in a timely manner to finish.

54. B: A student's IEP team does determine his/her eligibility for an alternate curriculum program. These programs are not the first choice for students with disabilities (A) and are not preferred over general curricula with accommodations and/or modifications (C). Rather, if an individual student still finds the general education curriculum too demanding even with accommodations and modifications provided, then an alternate curriculum program is a placement to consider. Students in these programs are typically assigned to a special education classroom as their primary placement but may also attend some general education classes and enrichment activities during the school day to interact with students without disabilities (D).

55. A: According to Piaget, elementary-school-age children are in the stage of concrete operations. They can understand mental operations and their reversibility for the first time. Piaget said that children develop certain conservation skills earlier and others later. Conservation of number develops earliest, usually around ages five to seven years. The children in this question have mild developmental delays. So it can be expected that some of them may have developed this understanding and some have not. This would be a good task to offer them at their age. Therefore, option A is correct.

Class inclusion is typically acquired around the age of seven or eight. These children are only six and also have mild developmental delays, so they may be a year or two behind other children in cognitive development. In tests with the 20-questions game, children six to eight with normal cognitive development would simply guess (e.g., "Is it a banana?"), whereas children aged nine to eleven would think in terms of categories (e.g., "Is it something you eat?"), showing the ability of classification. A class inclusion task for six-year-olds with mild developmental delays would be too advanced, and they would probably all fail at it. Therefore, option B is incorrect.

Conservation of weight usually develops around the ages of nine to ten. This would be beyond the development of cognitively average six-year-olds, let alone those with mild developmental delays. Therefore, option C is incorrect.

Conservation of volume is typically attained around the ages of twelve to fourteen, according to Piaget. It would be far beyond the cognitive abilities of six-year-olds. Therefore, option D is incorrect.

56. A: Music is a good reinforcement for maintaining and increasing desired behaviors, as Gary loves it. Setting music to play when he wheels his chair would reinforce his doing it. Therefore, option A is correct.

Setting music to play when the chair's wheels turn would not selectively reinforce the desired behavior of Gary wheeling his own chair. The wheels turn when anyone pushes his chair. The music would also reinforce his letting others push him, which he already does. Gary's team wants to decrease this and replace it with self-mobility. Presenting the same reinforcement for both behaviors will neither increase self-mobility nor decrease waiting for others to push him. Therefore, option B is incorrect.

This goal cannot be achieved in the single step of wheeling all the way down the hall. The goal will be achieved gradually and in much smaller increments, as Gary wheels his chair a few feet at a time. Eventually, with the reinforcement of music, he may propel his chair longer distances. Withholding music for not performing an action he cannot learn in one step would be an overly-restrictive punishment and would not be effective. Therefore, option C is incorrect.

Playing music all the time is not indicated even though Gary loves it. If it is not associated with the desired behavior, then it will not reinforce that behavior. In addition, presenting a constant stimulus results in habituation (one stops noticing it) or over-stimulation (it becomes aversive). Encouragement and praise could be effective, but the question gives no information regarding how Gary responds to either of these. Verbal praise alone may not be as effective as music. Praise paired with music for self-mobility could be effective. Therefore, option D is incorrect.

57. C: Wyatt cannot write but can use his fists, so a computer touch screen is a good way for him to record his test answers. This is a good example of adapting lessons; therefore, option A is incorrect.

Fabian cannot take a test visually, so his teacher has provided recorded questions, and he presses buttons to record his answers. This is a good example of adapting lessons; therefore, option B is incorrect.

Sue cannot see as well as other students in her class and cannot use a pen as well as others, yet she is taking a pen and paper test despite her visual and manual disabilities. This is not a good example of adapting lessons; therefore, option C is correct.

Donnie cannot hear the sound of a fire alarm, but the school has added strobe lights, which he can see, so he can participate in fire drills. This is a good example of adaptive education; therefore, option D is incorrect.

58. C: Medicating Bart due to his anxiety is not a good idea. Nothing was stated about his having an anxiety disorder. Anxiety about such a big change would be natural in many students. Despite his accomplishments Bart may lack confidence or he may simply feel threatened by change. This is situational anxiety, not organic anxiety, and drugs are not the answer in this case. Therefore option A is incorrect.

Putting off the move is counterproductive since Bart is ready now in terms of his skills. His anxiety over a big change is unlikely to go away simply by delaying the move. Therefore option B is incorrect.

Bart's teacher can teach him various coping skills specifically aimed at managing transitions such as this. Once he learns these strategies, he is likely to feel more equipped to deal with changes and with the feelings of anxiety they provoke. Therefore option C is correct.

Forcing the move and ignoring Bart's anxiety is like throwing an unwilling child who cannot swim into a swimming pool to force the child to adapt or drown. It is likely to be traumatic. Such a decision is also unnecessary since Bart's teacher can help him feel more prepared before the move by teaching him coping skills. Therefore option D is incorrect.

59. D: Although all of these choices may benefit Corey to a certain extent, providing one-to-one intervention in reading fluency is most likely to improve his reading fluency. One-to-one instruction allows Corey to move at his own pace and move on to the next skill when he has mastered the previous skill. This allows the teacher to truly meet Corey's needs in reading fluency and give him complete attention during the intervention time. Answer A is incorrect because a student with a severe deficiency in reading fluency likely needs additional intervention outside the classroom. Answer B is incorrect because a small group would not allow Corey to work at his own pace and provide the individual instruction that he may need. Answer C is incorrect because modifying the material will not allow Corey to build his reading fluency skills.

60. B: Students tend to remember vocabulary words when they have some kind of visual to associate with the word. Many students that struggle with vocabulary words often need a lot of practice in understanding these new words, so giving them multiple methods to learn the words is beneficial. Simply telling the students what words to memorize often does not work with students with disabilities that struggle with vocabulary. Answer A is incorrect because providing a multisensory model may be helpful for some students but is not the most effective method of learning new vocabulary. Answer C is incorrect because additional vocabulary quizzes might become too overwhelming for some students. Answer D is incorrect because although a dictionary can help learn the term at first, this strategy will not likely be effective in the long term.

61. B: Although all these choices can be helpful strategies for students who are at risk, providing a caring and supportive classroom environment is most likely to be effective. Many of these students do not have much positive support in their lives and need someone that they can trust and rely on. Although it may be difficult for these students to open up and talk, it is important that they have a caring classroom setting and someone that they can turn to when they need to talk. Answer A is incorrect because simply giving them accommodations may not provide them with enough support to be successful. Answer C is incorrect because requiring peer collaboration without a supportive climate may not be effective for students who are hesitant to engage. Answer D is incorrect because providing opportunities for after-school activities does not directly influence the classroom climate.

62. C: Guided practice involves students working together or with the assistance of the teacher. The purpose of implementing guided practice into the lesson plan, especially for students with disabilities, is to ensure that they understand the material by guiding them through it. Rather than just asking them to do the work by themselves right away, they can get some support from the teacher or their classmates. Answer A is incorrect because this would be an example of independent practice. Answer B is incorrect because this would be an example of teacher feedback rather than guided practice. Answer D is incorrect because teachers modeling the instruction would still be part of the instruction.

63. A: In order for a student like Jessica to succeed in the general education setting, it is likely best to differentiate the learning environment. One way to do this would be to create a space in the classroom where there are no distractions. This way, Jessica can still access the content of her peers while being free from distractions that might impact her ability to learn. Answer B is incorrect because differentiating the content would not be appropriate; she can still learn what the other students learn. Answer C is incorrect because differentiating the process would not be appropriate; she can still learn the content in the same way that the other students learn. Answer D is incorrect because differentiating the product would not be appropriate; she can be assessed using the same methods as other students.

64. C: Although all these choices may be appropriate for certain students, researching the high school offerings would be considered the most appropriate in supporting the immediate transition into high school. Answer A is incorrect because while career exploration is valuable, this would not aid in the immediate transition into high school. Answer B is incorrect because researching colleges is less immediately relevant when transitioning into high school. Answer D is incorrect because although independent skills may be important, researching high school class offerings would be more immediately relevant as a transition activity for eighth grade students.

65. D: All students can benefit from movement activities as a method of stimulating their brain, so incorporating this strategy for all students would be the most beneficial. Although it may not always be possible each class period, finding creative ways to get Zachary up and moving with the rest of the class will make him feel less singled out. It is important to develop a plan for when these movement breaks are needed for students like Zachary and how they can be implemented for the entire class. Answer A is incorrect because Zachary may take advantage of the pass system and use it more than he really needs to. Answer B is incorrect because giving him a timer also might become a distraction to Zachary and other students around him. Answer C is incorrect because giving a student his own area might end up making him feel singled out.

66. C: Instructional scaffolding can be a useful tool in teaching students with disabilities because it provides extra support to ensure that the students are comprehending the lesson. Many students with disabilities struggle to understand or engage in the lesson that a teacher is giving. Instructional scaffolding helps these students by connecting learning to previous knowledge or by easing the students into the new learning. Answer A is incorrect because providing an alternate method of learning would be an example of changing the lesson to meet the needs of the student. Answer B is incorrect because multisensory approaches tend to occur after the lesson has been taught. Answer D is incorrect because students are provided the same amount of instruction when the lesson is scaffolded, just at a slower pace.

67. A: Early intervention services are designed to help young children who are struggling with basic skills. Speech or communication issues are common in younger children who struggle with talking or understanding. Early intervention services are important to identify the areas that need to be targeted right away in children. Answer B is incorrect because academic services would typically come after the student has worked on early intervention skills. Answer C is incorrect because counseling services wouldn't likely begin until students were older. Answer D is incorrect because adaptive services would likely apply to older students who struggle with everyday functions.

68. C: Students can be at risk for many reasons, and drug and alcohol abuse can be one of them. It is important to seek out help for these students while also providing them support at the same time. These kinds of issues must be reported in order to get the students the help they need because of the impact substance use can have on their lives and futures. By working with a counselor to address her substance use and related stressors, Courtney will be able to focus better on her schoolwork. Answer A is not the best first step because the teacher should begin by referring Courtney to the school counselor or other support staff, who are trained to assess risk and coordinate appropriate services, including parent involvement when appropriate. Answer B is incorrect because taking her to a rehabilitation facility may be overstepping the boundaries of a teacher. Answer D is incorrect because students who have admitted to or are suspected of using drugs and alcohol must be reported in order to get them the help they need.

69. D: Practicing doing laundry every once in a while and in a separate location from where the skill was learned provides maintenance and generalization. This allows the student an opportunity to remember how to practice the skill but also complete it across various settings. Maintenance and generalization are important instructional strategies in providing opportunities for students to practice skills. Answer A is incorrect because practicing the skill every day in the same location does not provide maintenance or generalization. Answer B is incorrect because practicing the skill in the same location it was learned does not provide generalization. Answer C is incorrect because maintenance is typically demonstrated with less frequent practice.

70. A: Embodied learning allows students to participate in activities that get the whole body involved. It allows students to move while still learning the content. Many students struggle to sit and learn all day, so this kind of instruction allows them to get up and move. It is important to provide a variety of learning activities in order to meet the needs of all of the students in the class. Answer B is incorrect because inquiry-based learning involves having students ask questions in order to learn. Answer C is incorrect because blended learning involves a combination of online and traditional learning. Answer D is incorrect because service learning typically involves students going out into the community to learn.

71. D: A spiraling curriculum involves revisiting key concepts throughout instruction in increasing complexity and depth, building upon previous learning. Reviewing material in the same way as it was initially taught (A) doesn't involve progression. Completing homework in advance (B) does not involve revisiting content with increased complexity. While implementing visual and auditory explanations (C) might be useful, it is not an example of spiraling curriculum.

72. B: For a class such as math, which tends to be book heavy and involves a lot of the work using the textbook, the most beneficial strategy to use for this student would be an audio version of the textbook. This way, the student can listen to the problems instead of reading them. Answer A is incorrect because although a modified assignment length may be helpful, it may not be necessary if the student is completing the entire assignment. Answer C is incorrect because although preferential seating might be helpful, it likely will not have as much of an impact as having access to the audio book. Answer D is incorrect because although having extended time may also help, it may or may not be accessed based on the needs of the student.

73. C: It is incorrect that using both visual and auditory input (C) distracts or confuses students with learning disabilities. The information is reinforced for them when presented in both sensory modalities. Special educators find that students' reading comprehension can improve dramatically when spoken language is presented along with printed language (A). They also find that students with reading learning disabilities, who typically read slowly and laboriously, can increase their reading speed just as dramatically when the auditory version is added to the visual (B). Therefore, it is correct that using visual and auditory input together is more effective than either sensory modality alone (D).

74. B: Suggest new and innovative ways students can use their journals including automatic writing, found poetry, lists, and collages. While journals are intensely personal and should never be read without the student's permission, teachers can certainly inspire students to use the journals to explore their ideas in innovative ways.

75. C: Any kind of observational assessment will involve direct observation of Keith's behavior, which is what the teacher wants to evaluate. If the teacher uses the same recording methods as for behavioral baseline measures, comparing current results to baseline can indicate Keith's progress. Norm-referenced tests (A) are standardized tests and typically measure academic achievement, not behavior. Interviewing Keith (B) is contraindicated because he has expressive language deficits and may have difficulty responding, and also because observing what the student does is more accurate than asking the student to describe his own behavior. Curriculum-based testing (D) connects assessment to instruction. While behavioral interventions have probably been incorporated during Keith's classroom instruction, curriculum-based assessments are related to curriculum content areas, not behavioral issues.

76. A: Instructional level. In one minute, a student who reads with 95–100% accuracy is at an independent reading level. A student who reads with 90–95% accuracy is at an instructional level. A student who reads with less than 90% accuracy is at a frustration level.

77. A: Norm-referenced tests compare the student's score to norms, such as national averages of scores for students of the same age or grade level. These are standardized tests, such as national achievement tests including the SAT, ACT, GRE, etc. Criterion-referenced tests (B) do not compare students' scores to other students' scores, but rather measure students' performance against a criterion, standard, or objective previously determined and given to students before testing. Class quizzes, exams, oral reports, presentations, experiments, and performance-based tests (C) are examples of criterion-referenced tests. Ipsative measures or tests (D) compare the student's performance to their own previous performance.

78. B: These students might be unable to locate errors in their own work. This is the only logical answer. Answers A, C, and D do not make sense in context.

79. A: Norm-referenced tests are based on the bell-shaped curve of a normal distribution. These reference tests are designed to place students in a percentile compared to other students of similar demographics. As opposed to criterion-referenced tests, which are not competitive, norm-referenced tests are based not only on what a student knows, but on what they know compared to other students. While these tests will not determine whether a student passes or fails a grade, they can provide educators with an indication of the student's weaknesses and strengths. Additionally, these tests are often used for college admissions.

80. D: The Leiter is a completely nonverbal IQ test. It would be appropriate for a nonverbal student. Therefore option A is not correct.

Raven's Progressive Matrices is another nonverbal IQ test. It would also be a good choice for a nonverbal student. Therefore option B is not correct.

The TONI-III is the third edition of the Test of Nonverbal Intelligence. It is also used to assess intelligence in nonverbal students. Therefore option C is not correct.

The Stanford-Binet is a mixed verbal/nonverbal battery that still places significant demands on language compared with fully nonverbal tests. For a completely nonverbal deaf student, specialized nonverbal measures like the Leiter, Raven's, or TONI are preferred, making the Stanford-Binet the least appropriate choice among the options, without asserting that it categorically requires hearing, speaking, reading, and writing for all subtests. Therefore option D is correct.

81. C: A standard deviation of 15 means that scores typically will vary, or deviate, around the mean, or average, within 15 points. The difference between Mia's and Cara's scores is only 6 points. This does not necessarily indicate that Mia has a higher IQ than Cara. Therefore option A is incorrect.

Mia's score was 125 on a test whose mean is 100. This means she scored above the average for this test. Cara's score was 119. This means she also scored above the average for this test. Therefore option B is incorrect.

Both Cara and Mia scored above the average of 100 on this test. Therefore option C is correct.

Cara and Mia both scored more than one standard deviation, or 15 points, above the average of 100 for this test. They did not have average scores but rather, above-average scores. Therefore option D is incorrect.

82. A: Diagnostic assessments are primarily used to determine a student's current instructional level and identify areas of strength and need. Diagnostic data can influence instructional decisions, but specific decisions about disability identification and special education services require more comprehensive evaluations beyond a single diagnostic assessment. Answer B is incorrect because the diagnostic assessment alone would not be able to determine what disability a student may have. Answer C is incorrect because although the diagnostic assessment can assist in determining the special education services for a student, it likely would not be the only measure used. Answer D is incorrect because a summative assessment would be more appropriate to determine how much a student has learned.

83. B: The results of achievement tests are often used in conjunction with other factors to aid in determining eligibility for a specific learning disability. Achievement tests assess the academic achievement of students and compare those scores with students of a similar age. The results of the test aid in determining whether the student is having significant academic difficulties and requires special education services. Answer A is incorrect because intelligence tests are used to determine the cognitive ability of a student, which is not as directly related to academic achievement as an achievement test. Answer C is incorrect because a screening test would be used before the achievement test to determine whether achievement testing was necessary. Answer D is incorrect because curriculum-based tests are typically used to monitor the progress of students.

84. D: Although all these methods may be helpful in measuring a student's behavior needs, using random time samples can be beneficial in determining the frequency of the behavior. Random time samples allow teachers to observe the student at various times throughout the day to determine the cause and frequency of these behaviors. This can be measured to determine how much progress the student is making on their goals. Answer A is incorrect because curriculum-based measures tend to be more effective for students with academic goals. Answer B is incorrect because it may be difficult to measure how a student compares to their peers. Answer C is incorrect because simply counting the number of referrals likely does not provide sufficient data.

85. D: Although it can certainly be beneficial to perform a cognitive screening on students, these typically come a little later than kindergarten. Many students in kindergarten are still developing, so a cognitive screening does not always provide the best results. These screening assessments are designed to determine what areas students are struggling with, but they can only be useful for age-appropriate activities. Answer A is incorrect because communication screenings can be valuable in determining how well students interact with others. Answer B is incorrect because hearing and vision screenings are important in helping to determine the cause of a student's struggles. Answer C is incorrect because many kindergarten students struggle with motor skills, which may impact their ability to learn.

86. C: For students with specific learning disabilities, it is important that they are able to access standardized tests to determine what kind of progress they are making. In order for them to access these tests, oftentimes they will need to be provided accommodations. These accommodations allow them to access the same test as their general education peers. Answer A is incorrect because alternative tests are typically for students who cannot access the standardized test even with accommodations. Answer B is incorrect because standardized tests do not typically allow modifications to the tests. Answer D is incorrect because differentiation would be an example of something that would be done in a classroom setting rather than on a standardized test.

87. C: In order to allow a student with a learning disability in reading comprehension to access summative assessments, it is best practice to provide accommodations. Summative assessments are designed to assess what a student has learned at the end of a specified unit, so it is important that they are properly assessed. Students with reading comprehension deficiencies, however, will need to access accommodations such as oral presentation of the text. Answer A is incorrect because alternate assessments are typically reserved for students with significant cognitive disabilities, so this is likely too extreme of an option for Tristan. Answer B is incorrect because students with learning disabilities typically do not access assessments with modifications. Answer D is incorrect because informal assessments are typically used for formative assessments.

88. D: Alternate assessments must be based on grade-level standards for students. Alternate assessments are created for students who are unable to participate in general assessments with accommodations. Answer A is incorrect because most students who receive special education services take the general assessment. Answer B is incorrect because although many students who take the alternate test do not receive a high school diploma, this is not always the case. Answer C is incorrect because the decision about alternate testing is typically up to the IEP team based on the needs of the student.

89. B: Screening tests can be valuable in that they provide information in determining whether or not additional assessments should be conducted. These screening tests are typically used on students who struggle in a particular area in order to determine whether or not they should be assessed further in that area. Oftentimes, screening tests can determine whether or not a special education evaluation should be conducted. Answer A is incorrect because a screening test would typically be given in order to determine whether or not a student should be evaluated for special education services. Answer C is incorrect because these screening tests cannot show progress on IEP goals. Answer D is incorrect because placement tests are typically separate from these kinds of screening tests.

90. C: When students fall within one standard deviation of the mean, this is most often considered in the average range, and a student would not be eligible. Students being evaluated for a specific learning disability must have a score that is considered statistically significant in order to be eligible. It is important to understand where one standard deviation falls in order to determine where the student scores. Answer A is incorrect because the student would likely not be eligible unless they were outside one standard deviation. Answer B is incorrect because although it is possible that more testing could be considered, this score shows that the student is within the average range. Answer D is incorrect because there is likely not enough information to determine whether or not a 504 Plan would be appropriate for Joseph.

91. A: One of the challenges of identifying students who receive English learner services for special education is deciding whether or not their needs are related to a disability. It can be difficult to distinguish between a student with a disability and a student who is new to the language. It is crucial to take all of the steps that are necessary to ensure the correct placement of these students. Answer B is incorrect because if it is determined that a student is eligible for special education services, the IEP must meet their needs. Answer C is incorrect because special education services would be beneficial in providing the student access to the general education curriculum. Answer D is incorrect because the decision is based on whether or not services are needed for special education rather than the services they already received.

92. D: Curriculum-based assessments can be beneficial in determining how much progress a student is making on their goals. It is important to monitor the progress a student is making by giving them curriculum-based assessments that are directed toward their IEP goals. These data can help to guide instruction and determine if any changes need to be made so that the student makes continued progress toward that goal. Answer A is incorrect because comparing a student's score to others in the district would be a norm-referenced or standardized assessment. Answer B is incorrect because comparing a student's score to their grade in the class would likely be a summative assessment. Answer C is incorrect because comparing a student's score to the average score would likely be a norm-referenced assessment.

93. C: Although it could be beneficial to conduct a verbal intelligence test on all these students, it would be most appropriate for a student with a writing disability. Students who struggle with communication, including writing, often struggle to express themselves. The verbal intelligence test measures this in order to determine if there are supports that can be put in place for students with these deficits. Answer A is incorrect because students with intellectual disabilities could struggle with these kinds of assessments, and other assessments would be more appropriate for reevaluating special education services. Answer B is incorrect because although students with math deficiencies may struggle with verbal intelligence, students who struggle with reading and writing are more likely to benefit from these tests. Answer D is incorrect because students with visual impairments will likely have a separate kind of assessment to measure their abilities in this area when reevaluating for special education services.

94. A: When assessing a student for fine motor skills, it is important to take a look at activities such as drawing, writing, and using scissors. These kinds of skills are considered fine movements in that they are smaller movements that involve the hands, wrists, fingers, or toes. These kinds of assessments are important for determining whether or not a student needs additional support with a skill such as handwriting. Answer B is incorrect because while watching a student making numbers with their hands can be a form of fine motor assessment, it is not as relevant to the fine motor skills needed in a classroom setting as drawing a picture would be. Answer C is incorrect because watching a student throw a ball would be looking at gross motor abilities. Answer D is incorrect because watching a student riding a bike would also be looking at gross motor skills.

95. A: Standardized assessment tests, examining areas of weakness in student work to determine patterns, teacher observations, and interviews with the student are the typical steps taken to identify specific skill deficits in math. After this, the teacher should be well-prepared to plan instruction.

96. A: The goal of a summative assessment is to evaluate what a student has learned over a specific topic or topics. Summative assessments are typically graded and may include some kind of a test or paper that the students are responsible for. Summative assessments can be valuable for students with disabilities for many reasons, including assessing a student's progress on IEP goals or whether or not a student's supports have been beneficial. Answer B is incorrect because determining appropriate instruction would be considered a diagnostic assessment. Answer C is incorrect because monitoring student learning would be considered a formative assessment. Answer D is incorrect because comparing students to a norm would be considered a norm-referenced or standardized assessment.

97. B: The Education for All Handicapped Children Act, or Education for the Handicapped Act (EHA), was passed in 1975 (Public Law #94-142) to guarantee everyone with disabilities aged 5–21 a free appropriate public education, or FAPE (C). It stated that all students with disabilities must be educated as much as possible in the least restrictive environment, or LRE (D). In 1990, this law was reauthorized and renamed the Individuals with Disabilities Education Act, or IDEA (A). It was later amended in successive reauthorizations in 1991, 1997, and 2004.

98. A: Although all these strategies can be beneficial in overcoming cultural biases, learning why the bias occurs is likely to be the most effective. If teachers are able to analyze and understand why some of the biases occur, they may be able to eliminate them or overcome them. Cultural biases occur for many reasons, but it is important to understand the impact that a teacher has and what the needs of the student might be. Answer B is incorrect because being objective may not be quite as effective as showing empathy for certain students. Answer C is incorrect because not all students will likely learn the same way, so they should not necessarily be treated the same. Answer D is incorrect because simply encouraging these cross-group interactions may or may not help in overcoming personal biases.

99. A: Whichever professional is best able to explain what the student's test results imply for the student's education should interpret those results for the IEP team members. It could be the student's special education teacher, who will be an IEP team member (B); it could be the school psychologist, who may or may not be on the student's IEP team (C); or it could be another professional who is not on the IEP team (D), because being a member of the IEP team is not required for this function. The important factor is the ability to relate assessment results to educational planning and programming that will address needs and strengths identified in those results.

100. D: The National Council on Disability is an independent federal agency that makes recommendations to the President and Congress regarding issues related to disabilities. The FCSN (A) is an organization founded in Boston, Massachusetts that informs, helps, and supports parents of children with disabilities, involved professionals, and communities. The CPAS (B), formed by the University of California, San Francisco (UCSF) through a grant from the National Institute on Disability and Rehabilitation Research (NIDRR), supplies research, dissemination, training, and technical help with personal assistance services concerns nationwide. The NDRN (C) represents the needs of its members in Protection and Advocacy (P&A) before federal agencies and Congress, but is not itself a federal agency and does not make recommendations to the president.

101. B: An Individualized Education Program is a requirement of law. The plan, written by a team of individuals including the classroom teacher, the special education teacher, parents or guardians, the student (if appropriate), and other interested individuals, establishes objectives and goals and offers a timeline in which to reach them.

102. D: Begin by welcoming the mother and discussing her son's academic improvements. Assure her that the teachers, the mother, and the child share goals for the student's success. Explain the behavior problems and ask if the mother has insights to share. It's important to keep communication open.

103. A: The Americans with Disabilities Act. The ADA is a federal act prohibiting discrimination based on disability in the areas of employment, state and local government, public accommodations, commercial facilities, transportation and telecommunications.

104. A: Special education classrooms, once attended throughout the day by students with disabilities, are being used less frequently. Many students with disabilities are now in regular classrooms and may only spend a portion of their time in a special education classroom. This is also true for students with learning disabilities. Depending on the severity of the disability, a student may visit the special education room for a short period of time each day to receive additional support in his or her area of weakness. English and math are the most common subjects that students go to special education classrooms to receive instruction or help in.

105. C: The Family Educational Rights and Privacy Act of 1974 protects student records. Under this legislation, parents (and eligible students once rights transfer at age 18 or upon attendance at a postsecondary institution) have the right to inspect and review the student's education records, and schools generally may not disclose these records to others without written consent, except in specific circumstances allowed by law (e.g., to school officials with a legitimate educational interest). Additionally, students have the opportunity to review their academic records and if necessary, make amendments in the instance of incorrect information. Information pertaining to the students' social security number, grades, grade point average, and academic performance are protected by this legislation, as well as information about behavioral issues such as suspensions, academic dishonesty, and probation.

106. B: Telling Nina simply to avoid the public library does not help to fulfill the goal of inclusion. It puts additional limits on a student who already has a disability. Restricting her library activities to the school does not give Nina the least restrictive environment. Therefore option A is incorrect.

The special education teacher should know how to foster respectful, beneficial relationships with professionals in the community. By supervising Nina she can aid her in using the public library while keeping her from disturbing the quiet and annoying the librarian. Teaching her to control the volume of her voice when she is in the public library may enable Nina to visit the library by herself in the future without disturbing the peace. Acting as a facilitator can change the librarian's negative attitude toward Nina and establish more friendly relations. This will eliminate the librarian's discrimination against Nina and will promote a more positive relationship between a student with a disability and a community professional. Therefore option B is correct.

Complaining to the principal is not taking responsibility as a teacher for collaborating with members of the community. Though the librarian is discriminating, complaining to the principal is a negative action. The school principal could not do anything beneficial unless he supervised Nina's library visits, which is a better role for the teacher to take. If he simply insisted to the librarian that she allow Nina to visit, the librarian would be further antagonized. Therefore option C is incorrect.

Sending Nina to the school psychologist for consolation would not change the situation itself. Counseling would be more appropriate for a situation that cannot be changed (i.e., to accept the fact that she has a disability). Therefore option D is incorrect.

107. C: Educating general education teachers and other school and community personnel about why Tina wears a helmet would clear up their misconceptions. Additionally, asking them to relay what they have learned to others would further dispel ignorance and discrimination. Therefore, option C is correct. (Note: We are assuming here that this would be done using ethical practices for confidential communication.)

Recommending that Tina not wear the helmet would result in endangering her, which would be irresponsible. Therefore, option A is incorrect.

To recommend that another person constantly accompany Tina rather than have her wear a helmet would be impractical or impossible. It would also be more restrictive. Wearing a helmet may look unusual, but it affords Tina more independence than would having a constant companion, even if this could be arranged. Therefore, option B is incorrect.

If Tina has the ability, it is a good idea for her to know how to explain to others, if she chooses, why she wears a helmet. However, telling her that it is her sole responsibility is an unfair burden. She is only one student dealing with the entire school and community. Since teachers and other personnel assist students with disabilities as needed, she can benefit from their assistance in this regard. Therefore, option D is incorrect.

108. A: A special education teacher should know how to serve as a resource person for families. By finding a group to fix Carly's chair at no charge, the teacher does this. Therefore, option A is correct.

Serving as a resource person for her student's family is part of the teacher's job. Therefore, option B is incorrect.

Paying for the repair herself is inappropriate. It is also unrealistic given a teacher's salary. It could make Carly's parents feel uncomfortable as well. And if there is a group that makes free repairs, it is an unnecessary expenditure. Therefore, option C is incorrect.

A charitable donation of a free chair sounds good, but the question states that Carly is not happy without her own chair. She is accustomed to it and is uncomfortable in the loaner chair. A donated chair is not the same as having the chair she is used to, and it might also be uncomfortable. It would be better to repair the chair that she likes. Therefore, option D is incorrect.

109. A: A behavior intervention plan is required to be updated at least once a year at the annual IEP meeting. Although there is no timeframe for when the behavior intervention plan must be implemented other than the annual IEP meeting, it is important to monitor. When students exhibit new behaviors or change behavior patterns, it might be time to make an update. Other students may not need updates more than once per year. Each student has different needs, and it is vital that each member of the team takes part in monitoring the student and their plan.

110. A: It is a requirement to hold a manifestation determination meeting whenever students with disabilities are subjected to a disciplinary change of placement. This is to ensure that the student is not being disciplined simply because he or she has a disability. If the behavior is not a manifestation of the student's disability, then the student will receive the same punishment as any other general education students. Answer B is incorrect because these students can be suspended for more than 10 days if it is not a manifestation of their disability. Answer C is incorrect because discipline may be different depending on the manifestation results. Answer D is incorrect because services can still be provided to students who get expelled from school.

111. A: Although all of these agencies may be beneficial for certain students based on their individual needs, school-to-work agencies would likely provide the most direct help for students with learning disabilities obtaining and maintaining jobs.

112. A: The communication plan is important for students with hearing impairments to describe the services that students like Marie will receive to access the curriculum. The communication plan describes the support available for students and the strategies that are used to communicate with others. The communication plan also lists the devices and assistive technology that these students may access. Answer B is incorrect because the annual goals describe which areas the student will focus on and be monitored in. Answer C is incorrect because the accommodations will list specific supports that will be put in place for the student to access the curriculum. Answer D is incorrect because the special factors section simply lists whether or not the student accesses the communication plan.

113. B: Although schools will do everything they can to provide students with disabilities the best possible education, this is not stated in the law. Schools must provide an appropriate education to students with disabilities, but this does not require maximizing best possible outcomes. It is important to ensure that students are receiving FAPE and have access to general education and special education services. The other options are components of FAPE.

114. C: Although parents may discuss some of the issues they have with their child's attendance at the IEP meeting, this is not typically discussed at the meeting. Differences that arise from the IEP meeting will typically stem from the IEP itself. Because there is no section in the IEP that specifically discusses attendance issues, this is the least likely issue to arise. Answer A is incorrect because it is common for the parents and teacher to have differences with regard to the student's IEP goals. Answer B is incorrect because parents may disagree about some of the accommodations that their child has access to. Answer D is incorrect because some parents may also have differences of opinion regarding the service delivery section of the IEP.

115. B: One of the most effective ways that special education teachers can support the parents of students with disabilities is to make sure that they stay informed. Holding meetings regularly on different topics can give the parents the tools they need to make their own decisions on what might be best for their child. This can also give them an opportunity to speak to other parents with disabled children to discuss strategies that they have used. Answer A is incorrect because just giving them a list of facts likely wouldn't be as meaningful as holding meetings in which they can ask questions. Answer C is incorrect because having them come in to shadow their son likely wouldn't help them with strategies they can use at home. Answer D is incorrect because it can be tricky to give them a list of providers without knowing their financial and healthcare situations.

116. D: Students who receive special education services at the high school level no longer access these services when they graduate, but they can access 504 Plans. These plans are designed to provide accommodations to students with disabilities in college or beyond in the workplace. Although students with disabilities cannot continue to receive these special education services when they graduate high school, it is important for them to understand the types of support that are available to them. Answer A is incorrect because students who receive special education services most often do not also have a 504 Plan. Answer B is incorrect because students who exit from special education may or may not access a 504 Plan, but this is not required. Answer C is incorrect because students with 504 Plans are not entitled to special education services.

117. C: The prior written notice section of the IEP proposes changes that the team determines are necessary to provide free appropriate public education for the child with a disability. The prior written notice is often the last section of the IEP, and it describes the reason for the IEP meeting and the changes that were made. Although prior written notice must be provided prior to any change in special education services, it is also included as a section in the IEP. Answer A is incorrect because a notice of meeting would be an invitation to the parents for the IEP meeting. Answer B is incorrect because providing copies of parent rights typically has a separate section in the IEP. Answer D is incorrect because a separate form must be filled out to end special education services.

118. D: The school psychologist does not typically provide special education instruction. Answer A is incorrect because school psychologists will often provide mental health support to students. Answer B is incorrect because school psychologists are also often responsible for administering different kinds of tests, including IQ assessments. Answer C is incorrect because school psychologists can also assist special education teachers in training staff on implementing behavior support.

119. D: Parents have the right to access educational records, including IEPs, for students until they turn 18. Once a student turns 18, the parents no longer have the same rights and must request the records through the student. This is important when working with students with IEPs who go to college or transfer to a different school. Answer A is incorrect because these protections do not apply to private schools that do not receive public funding. Answer B is incorrect because there are cases in which the school can release these records without parental consent. Answer C is incorrect because parents do have the right to request educational records within a certain time period.

120. C: Although it may be a good idea to send home a note for some students, many times a note will get lost in the transition from school to home. It is important to make a good first impression, and it is not the best idea to take a chance on the note not making it to the parents. The first meeting or introduction as case manager is important due to the nature of the relationship that will occur with the student. Answer A is incorrect because calling them with an introduction is a great way to establish a connection with the parents. Answer B is incorrect because setting up a meeting, if done in a positive manner, can allow the parents and the teacher to get on the same page at the start. Answer D is incorrect because meeting them in person can always be an effective way to first get to know someone.

Practice Test #2

1. The ABC approach to behavior analysis stands for...

a. Alphabetical classifying
b. Analysis brings changes
c. Appropriate behavioral choices
d. Antecedent-behavior-consequence

2. A student with ___________ has a great deal of difficulty with the mechanical act of writing. She drops her pencil, cannot form legible letters and cannot decode what she has written.

a. A nonverbal learning disorder
b. Dyslexia
c. Dyspraxia
d. Dysgraphia

3. Howard Gardner's theory of multiple intelligences organizes learners into what types of intelligences?

a. Verbal-linguistic, mathematical, musically attuned, visual-spatial, body embraced, interpersonal, naturalistic, existential
b. Empathic, recessive, aggressive, assertive, dogmatic, apologetic, determined, elusive
c. Verbal-linguistic, logical-mathematical, musical, visual-spatial, bodily-kinesthetic, interpersonal, intrapersonal, naturalistic, existential
d. Dramatic, musical, verbal, mathematical, dance-oriented, sports-oriented, scientific, socially concerned

4. A high school student has been diagnosed with oppositional defiant disorder. Some of the manifestations of the diagnosis are:

a. He engages in obsessive and compulsive activities such as hand washing, counting, and ritualistic behaviors.
b. He is self-occupied, depressed, and disorganized. He keeps to himself, is considered odd by his classmates, and could be suicidal.
c. The student is overly occupied with others, defending them from imagined slights and determined they recognize his concern as real rather than psychotic.
d. He goes out of his way to annoy others, is defiant, and goes into childish rages in which he blames others.

5. Ms. Malone, who teaches in an elementary school, is informed that her class will include five students who have cerebral palsy this year. Of these five, two also have diagnoses of intellectual disabilities. Ms. Malone can expect that:

a. All five students will have very similar degrees of disability due to their cerebral palsy.
b. The two students with intellectual disabilities will have much greater special education needs than the three with only cerebral palsy.
c. The magnitude of the special education needs of the two students with intellectual disabilities should depend solely on their levels of intellectual disabilities.
d. The degrees of disability and special education needs of all five students could vary widely.

6. A student who has difficulty understanding spoken language has a deficit in:

a. Expressive communication
b. Receptive communication
c. Verbal communication
d. Social communication

7. A second grader finds it impossible to remain in her seat. She wanders around the room, sprawls on the floor and rolls back and forth when asked to do math problems, and jumps up and down when waiting in line. When the teacher tells her to sit down, she rolls her eyes in apparent disgust and looks to other students for support. When she finds a student looking back, she laughs and makes a face. The teacher has noticed that when a reward is attached to good behavior, the girl is consistently able to control her actions for long periods of time. But when reprimanded without the promise of a reward, she becomes angry and tearful. This child is most likely manifesting:

a. Tourette syndrome
b. Attention-deficit/hyperactivity disorder
c. Lack of sufficiently developed behavior and social skills
d. Psychosis

8. Cory is a fifth-grade student who suffers from attention deficit hyperactivity disorder (ADHD). Which of the following is most likely to co-occur with ADHD?

a. Learning disability
b. Speech impairment
c. Depression
d. Anxiety

9. James has severe cerebral palsy and is nonverbal and nonambulatory. He cannot read or write, but he has excellent receptive language skills and can answer yes/no questions. Due to severe contractures, he cannot use his fingers or hands functionally, but he can grasp an object inserted into his fist. You are ordering adaptive equipment for him. Which would be the best choice?

a. A communication board with a pointer
b. A computer with a keyboard
c. A voice-activated computer
d. An adaptive holder enabling him to manipulate a pen

10. Stephen has a very high IQ, but he must use a wheelchair and is almost completely immobilized except for limited use of one hand, with which he can only press buttons. His paralysis affects his vocal cords, so he cannot speak. Stephen excels in all academic subjects, most notably in the sciences and expressive and receptive language skills. His communication is limited by his disabilities. Which would be the most appropriate adaptive equipment for him in the classroom and elsewhere?

a. An adaptive pencil holder and paper holder, both attached to his wheelchair
b. A computer with a voice synthesizer that he can program to speak for him
c. An electrolarynx he can use for speech in place of his paralyzed vocal cords
d. A communication board with buttons he can press to select various words

11. Jan is a student transitioning from a residential facility to a community placement. She is nonverbal but can vocalize and uses a wheelchair. From a combination of intellectual disabilities and physical disabilities, she has not had bladder control and has been wearing a diaper. The doctor, nurses, and therapists have consulted, and they feel her physical condition should not prevent her from learning bladder control with training. One therapist got her an enuresis alarm, which is placed in her diaper and sounds when wet. This gives Jan and the staff a more immediate awareness of when urination occurs, but it does not make her independent. What is the next step that they teach her?

a. To try to control her bladder when she feels the urge to urinate
b. To raise her hand and vocalize when she feels wet
c. To vocalize when she hears the alarm sounding
d. To wheel herself to the bathroom before she urinates

12. What is NOT an environmental factor that could lead to positive student development?

a. Relationships with teachers
b. Structure in daily routine
c. Getting enough sleep
d. Having intelligent parents

13. William is autistic and is very proficient at computer programming. His teacher helped him to find a part-time computer job while he was still in high school. William has always lived at home with his parents. He will be attending community college classes following graduation from high school and continuing to work at his part-time job. He is interested in living on his own but is unsure about what he will need to know to accomplish this. How might his teacher best help him reach this goal?

a. Advise him to take a class in independent living skills along with his other classes.
b. Tell him about a free resource network's website that helps people make such transitions.
c. Tell him to try getting an apartment with a roommate and see how he likes it.
d. Advise him to stay at home with his parents until he is more prepared to move.

14. Ms. Wood is a new teacher. Her first class includes a number of students from urban and impoverished backgrounds. When she gives standardized tests, these students score lower on measures of vocabulary and logic. For example, with word pair completion, given the word "cup" and the choices of "saucer," "table," "fork," or "chair," these students choose "table" rather than "saucer." What is the explanation for this?

a. These students have no experience with a cup and saucer, so a cup sits directly on the table.
b. These students have impaired language development due to poor nutrition and deprivation.
c. These students have never been taught to make logical word associations by their parents.
d. These students do not recognize formal logic because they have never read books at home.

15. Which of the following is true of co-occurring conditions for students with ADHD who receive special education services?

a. Anxiety is the most common co-occurring disorder for students with ADHD.
b. Speech problems are more common in students without ADHD.
c. Almost half of students with ADHD also have a learning disability.
d. The majority of students with ADHD have conduct disorders.

16. Which of the following is a criticism of the humanism learning theory?

a. The theory does not account for internal influences.
b. The theory does not consider the social aspect of learning.
c. The theory is relative and does not provide right or wrong answers.
d. The theory does not clearly define inherent goodness.

17. Which of the following is NOT true with regard to English learners receiving special education services?

a. There are no tests to definitively rule out learning disabilities.
b. They typically exhibit a disability in their native language first.
c. They must have adequate learning before a determination can be made.
d. Background knowledge can be a factor in the determination.

18. Which one of the following disability categories is likely to have the greatest impact on individuals across their life span?

a. Developmental delays
b. Speech or language impairments
c. Multiple disabilities
d. Specific learning disabilities

19. When screening a student for potential deficiencies as a preschooler, which of the following would be considered typical emotional development?

a. Changing the rules of a game they play
b. Being rigid with daily routines
c. Wanting to be dependent on caregivers
d. Struggling to take turns with peers

20. Which of the following is generally the strongest environmental factor influencing whether an individual with a disability is able to achieve positive life outcomes?

a. The type of disability that the person has
b. The personality of the individual with the disability
c. The meaning of the disability to the individual
d. The support system that the individual has

21. Positive behavioral interventions are most likely to:

a. Control the problem behavior.
b. Suppress the problem behavior.
c. Replace the problem behavior.
d. Analyze the problem behavior.

22. Which of the following models used in planning instruction for students with disabilities is described as an example of "student-directed planning"?

a. The model and process of Group Action Planning (GAP)
b. The Choosing Options and Accommodations for Children (COACH) model
c. The model and process of Making Action Plans (MAPs)
d. The Planning Alternative Tomorrows with Hope (PATH) model

23. An intellectually disabled teen has been offered a job by an elderly neighbor. The neighbor wants the teen to work alongside her in the garden twice a week. They will plant seeds, transplant larger plants, weed, lay mulch, water, and fertilize. Later in the season, they will cut flowers and arrange bouquets, pick produce, and sell it all at the neighbor's roadside stand. The neighbor, the teen's mother, and the teen's special education teacher meet to discuss the proposal. The plan is:

a. Tentatively accepted. Because the teen is excited about having a job, her mother and teacher reluctantly agree. They both know the girl is likely to lose interest quickly, and they caution the neighbor that if she truly needs help, she may want to look elsewhere. However, no one wants to disappoint the girl, and they all decide the experience will be good for her.
b. Rejected. Despite the teen's insistence she can manage these tasks, her mother and teacher believe she cannot. They fear trying will set her up for failure.
c. Rejected. The teacher and her mother are very uncomfortable with the neighbor's offer. They suspect the elderly woman is simply lonely or may be a predator who has selected an intellectually disabled victim because such children are particularly vulnerable.
d. Enthusiastically accepted. The adults discuss a background check and the possibility the teen might discover gardening is not for her and want to quit. However, this is most likely to happen early in her employment, giving the neighbor sufficient time to find another helper.

24. A teacher has a child who does not volunteer in class. When the teacher asks the student a question the student can answer, she does so with as few words as possible. The teacher isn't sure how to best help the child. She should:

a. Leave the child alone. She is clearly very shy and will be embarrassed by having attention drawn to her. She is learning in her own way.
b. Ask two or three highly social children to include this girl in their activities. She is shy, and she probably won't approach them on her own.
c. Observe the child over the course of a week or two. Draw her into conversation and determine if her vocabulary is limited, if she displays emotional problems, or if her reticence could have another cause. Note how the child interacts with others in the class. Does she ever initiate conversation? If another child initiates, does she respond?
d. Refer her to the school counselor immediately. It is clear the child is suffering from either a low IQ or serious problems at home.

25. The desired outcomes a teacher places on their students can also be referred to as what?

a. Goals
b. Expectations
c. Rules
d. Procedures

26. What type of assertiveness is a teacher displaying when she clearly states her concerns and strives to correct negative behaviors?

a. Hostile assertiveness
b. Constructive assertiveness
c. Empathic assertiveness
d. Inflexible assertiveness

27. The emotional balance of a classroom can be upset by conflict. Appropriate methods for a teacher to use in handling conflict do NOT include:

a. Gathering information and recapping the situation
b. Allowing children to come up with a solution themselves
c. Letting the issue drop once a solution has been agreed upon
d. Dealing with the conflict calmly and with a quiet voice

28. What is the primary strategy for supporting students who prefer structured routines over dynamic schedules and who are upset by sudden changes?

a. Maintaining the same schedule as much as possible
b. Giving advance warning of changes, such as a visitor or school assembly
c. Allowing students who are likely to be upset to stay next to the teacher or a friend who can comfort them
d. Teaching relaxation techniques

29. Jimmy is a general education eighth-grade student who is starting to struggle in the area of math calculations. Which of the following is the next step for his teacher?

a. Referring Jimmy for special education services
b. Attempting accommodations inside the classroom
c. Contacting Jimmy's parents about getting a tutor
d. Offering to work with Jimmy after school

30. Richard is blind, has profound intellectual disabilities, and uses a wheelchair. He displays behaviors of constant head weaving and frequent hand clapping. What are some programs you might recommend for him?

a. Apply soft restraints to his head and hands to minimize or control these behaviors until he gets used to not doing them and stops.
b. Place noise-making objects like rattles, jingle bells, or tambourines in his hands to replace the clapping behavior.
c. Have the doctor examine him for a possible neurological problem that could explain the head weaving.
d. Give him a variety of sensory stimulation using sound, touch, taste, and smell, and do nothing about the head weaving.

31. Clyde is 16 years old, has visual impairment, and reads on a first-grade level. What would be a good choice of materials for his teacher to provide him?

a. Large-print books on subjects relevant to teens
b. Children's books, which have large print and simple text
c. Regular library books with a magnifying glass
d. Large-print books with subjects geared to teens but with simplified text

Refer to the following for question 32:

> Mrs. Minor is working on social skills with her high-school-level autism spectrum disorder class. Her students are all high functioning. They do not have difficulty being in crowded or noisy places. They are not averse to being around other people. Their needs involve learning appropriate behaviors in social interactions, initiating social interaction with others, and participating more fully in social activities. She is designing curricula to incorporate social skills across settings.

32. Which of these is the best example of some instructional activities she might plan?

a. Classroom practice for in-school conversations; assignments to practice family conversations at home; guided practice in conversations during a community outing
b. Classroom writing assignments and quizzes on social rules; going on a field trip and writing an essay about it upon returning to the classroom; reading a social skills handbook in class
c. Practicing taking turns at a community sports event; practicing orderly behavior at a public library; practicing following instructions at a community volunteer program
d. Completing written homework assignments on social events; keeping a record of their daily number and duration of interactions with family members; watching an educational TV program on social skills with their families

33. Jimmy's behaviors disrupt his classroom daily. What is the first step the teacher and other school staff should take?

a. Refer Jimmy to receive special education services for a conduct or behavior disorder.
b. Conduct a functional behavior analysis to determine the purpose(s) of the behaviors.
c. Transfer Jimmy to a separate classroom reserved for students with behavior problems.
d. Recommend to parents that Jimmy be placed in a special school for problem students.

34. Justin is a ninth-grade student with a specific learning disability in the area of reading comprehension. Which of the following strategies would be most effective in ensuring that he maintains his knowledge of a story?

a. Asking him to read the story three times in a row
b. Asking him to reread the story for homework
c. Asking him to reread the story each week
d. Asking him to quiz himself on the story

35. Which of the following best describes the goal of implementing a functional curriculum for students with disabilities?

a. To teach independent living skills to students
b. To teach communication skills to students
c. To teach basic subjects to students
d. To teach everyday tasks to students

36. Which of the following best describes the implications for teaching for those who follow the behaviorist learning theory?

a. The teacher communicates through positive or negative reinforcements.
b. The teacher provides an environment that promotes self-learning.
c. The teacher facilitates collaborative learning and group work.
d. The discovery of students' behavior is guided by the teacher.

37. Chad is a fifth-grade student with ADHD who needs active involvement to stay focused, but who enjoys being away from people. How can the use of a workspace in the corner of the class be best implemented in the classroom to be beneficial for Chad?

a. Chad can be sent to the corner when he becomes disruptive.
b. Chad can go to the corner when he has an assignment to work on.
c. Chad can go to the corner as a reward for good behavior after he finishes his work.
d. Chad can go to the corner when he needs a break.

38. David is a fourth-grade student who has been struggling with some of his behaviors. Which of the following frequent behaviors would be most concerning when observing David?

a. Using swear words with peers
b. Bragging to gain attention
c. Telling lies and being dishonest
d. Having disagreements with friends

39. Which of the following does NOT describe one of the methods that students with disabilities can use to access the general education curriculum?

a. Changing the content that they are taught
b. Changing the method in which they are taught
c. Changing the demonstration of what they have learned
d. Changing the environment in which they are taught

40. Which of the following is LEAST descriptive of the purpose of the co-teaching model applied to teaching English to seventh-grade students?

a. Co-teaching increases the amount of attention that students receive.
b. Co-teaching helps to share control of the classroom.
c. Co-teaching increases the amount of differentiation in instruction.
d. Co-teaching helps to provide multiple areas of expertise.

41. Which of the following is the primary benefit of using small-group pull-out instruction to provide IEP accommodations for high school students with disabilities?

a. Providing students access to their IEP accommodations
b. Allowing the students to ask questions
c. Reducing teacher workload by focusing instruction
d. Providing extra practice with reading, writing, and math

42. When working with students who struggle with managing their own behavior, which of the following would NOT be considered a positive behavior intervention?

a. Social-emotional strategies
b. Consequences
c. Self-regulatory strategies
d. Coping skills

43. Marissa is an 11th-grade student who accesses special education services as a student with autism spectrum disorder. Which of the following lesson plan elements would likely be most beneficial in meeting her needs in her math class?

a. Providing a cross-curricular curriculum
b. Providing multiple tasks to complete
c. Providing multiple choices
d. Providing hands-on instruction

44. Which of the following is the best example of how nonverbal communication can be used to manage student behavior?

a. Clapping hands or blowing a whistle when students are disruptive
b. Posting classroom rules and expected behaviors
c. Giving students stickers or other small rewards when they behave well
d. Moving around the room and standing near students during class

45. Max is a fourth-grade student with a visual impairment. Which of the following would be most appropriate in supplementing his math curriculum?

a. Reading the problems to him orally
b. Allowing him extra time to work
c. Providing opportunities for hands-on experiences
d. Allowing him to use a computer

46. When writing a behavior intervention plan, what is the purpose of preventive strategies?

a. Identifying the behaviors targeted for reduction or increase
b. Finding behaviors that serve the same purpose as the unwanted behaviors
c. Eliminating the triggers or events that lead to the behaviors
d. Teaching the individual skills needed to use tools

47. Which one of the following components is most important in attaining goals that are measurable?

a. Concrete evidence
b. Cost analysis
c. Clarified descriptions
d. Overarching objectives

48. A student with disabilities does not demonstrate certain adaptive life skills such as cleaning up a work area at school, but his parents report that he has done so at home for years. An ecological assessment finds he does not demonstrate these skills in any other settings. Which instructional procedure is most appropriate for this student?

a. Reteaching him these skills
b. Teaching skill generalization
c. Teaching skill maintenance
d. Teaching skill discrimination

49. Which of the following is correct about classroom modifications for students with disabilities?

a. Teachers rarely make incidental adaptations to address immediate problems.
b. Comprehensive plans for students with disabilities should include adaptations.
c. Classroom modifications made on the spot are unnecessary and inappropriate.
d. Teachers' intentional, planned adaptations are unlikely to meet student needs.

50. Which of the following is most accurate regarding grouping strategies for teaching disabled and diverse students using multilevel instructional techniques?

a. These are best taught to the whole class.
b. Small groups are the optimal arrangement.
c. Multilevel instruction is best used in pairs.
d. A range of grouping strategies can be used.

51. A ninth grade special education teacher is giving students strategies for taking a Maze test. There will be several paragraphs in which some words have been blanked out. There are five possible answers for each blank. The best approach is to:

a. Read all answers; mark out any that are illogical. 'Plug in' the remaining words and mark out those that are grammatically incorrect or do not sound right using context clues.
b. Read the first answer first. If it is logical and sounds grammatically correct, select that word and move on to the next question. If not, move to the second answer and repeat.
c. Cover the answers and try to guess what the correct word is. Look at the five choices. Select the one closest in meaning to the word guessed.
d. Do the questions that seem easier first. Look for a pattern and select the remaining words accordingly.

52. Which of the following is a metacognitive learning strategy that aids in transferring learning to new, real-world situations?

a. Repetition
b. Learning to learn
c. Memorization
d. Passive listening

53. A teacher notices that the majority of students in his class failed an assignment despite demonstrated effort. Which of the following is the best course of action?

a. Lower the expectations of the students and design easier assignments.
b. Provide additional scaffolding and teaching while maintaining expectations
c. Do not make any changes, as students should be operating outside of their comfort zones.
d. Remove expectations and allow students to work at their own paces and skill levels, facilitating a more natural approach.

54. Response to Intervention (RTI) is:

a. Parents, classroom teacher, special education teacher and other caring persons stage an intervention to express how a student's socially unacceptable behavior upsets them
b. An opportunity for a student to openly and freely respond to specific interventions without fear of reprimand
c. A multi-tiered system in which a student with academic difficulties receives research-supported interventions and ongoing progress monitoring.
d. A formal complaint lodged by a parent or guardian in response to what they consider an intrusion by a teacher into private matters

55. Ms. Harris has a special education classroom in a school with a multicultural population. This year her class includes Asian children, Native American children, and Hispanic children. The students have been placed in her class appropriately in terms of their types and severity of disabilities and educational levels. Knowing her students' cultural backgrounds, Ms. Harris has devised classroom strategies to facilitate their learning. Which of these is most likely one of her strategies?

a. Strictly enforcing individual work by each student and punishing cheating
b. Setting up collaborative learning group projects among all of the students
c. Assigning each student a turn at teaching the class to foster leadership
d. Setting up a high-stakes contest among the students and posting scores

56. Oscar is a young adult living in the community and attending a day habilitation training program. He has Down syndrome, and his IQ tests yield very low scores. However, he is cooperative and can follow directions. Due to his level of cognitive functioning, he needs intensive training and repeated prompting to complete any task with multiple steps. He also requires prompting to continue to work; he is not lazy, but he loses focus and forgets what to do. Oscar does not display maladaptive behaviors. He is normally passive and does not initiate many activities, but he is quite willing to do many tasks given the direction to do so. His caregivers and the team planning his IEP want to help Oscar gain some independence by learning employment skills. Which training program would be most suitable for him?

a. A sheltered workshop where he assembles product sample kits along with other disabled students, with periodic group supervision
b. A special warehouse program for people with disabilities doing a packing job with one-on-one supervision and ongoing verbal prompts to complete each step
c. A special education classroom where he applies labels to products and is monitored along with many other students by one teacher with occasional verbal prompts
d. A special education classroom where the teacher gives academic lessons and quizzes on job skills to the whole class

57. Ms. Blanchard has a special education classroom with computers for every student. She has combined learning basic computer skills with using the computers to achieve instructional objectives. How does she accommodate a blind student, a visually impaired student, and a student with impaired manual skills?

a. She excuses the student with blindness from using the computer, frequently comes to help the visually impaired student by reading smaller text to her, and has the student with impaired manual skills read the screen but excuses him from typing.
b. She reads the onscreen text aloud to the students with visual impairments and does the typing for the student with impaired manual skills, having him dictate his input to her.
c. She provides an alternative lesson recording for the students with visual impairments to listen to and helps the manually impaired student with hand-over-hand guidance.
d. She uses speaking computers and earphones for the student with visual impairments and a touch screen computer for the manually impaired student.

58. A special education teacher assigns his students a collaborative group project. Which strategy would be most effective to benefit all students in the group?

a. Assigning one student the task of compiling and presenting the group's work
b. Allowing students to volunteer to make contributions to the project
c. Leading the activities himself and directing what the students do
d. Assigning each student an equal number of duties related to the project

59. Which of the following instructional strategies is most appropriate when lecturing to a class that includes students with disabilities in a high school class?

a. Giving the students access to the presentation
b. Giving the students skeleton notes to fill in
c. Giving the students an exemption from taking notes
d. Giving the students a partner to take notes with

60. Ross is a third-grade student who receives special education services as a student with another health impairment due to ADHD. Which of the following strategies would likely be LEAST effective for Ross?

a. Providing extra thinking time when asking a question
b. Providing one-on-one math instruction
c. Providing a setting with fewer distractions
d. Providing a model to demonstrate the task

61. Which of the following checks for understanding would be most appropriate when teaching a small-group writing lesson to seventh graders?

a. Using whiteboards
b. Using self-assessments
c. Using cooperative learning
d. Using flip charts

62. Brian is a 12th-grade student with an intellectual disability. Which of the following would be the best example of a functional curriculum in his science class?

a. Learning how to conduct an experiment
b. Learning how to read a book about planets
c. Learning how to maintain a garden
d. Learning how to calculate speed

63. Cheyenne is an eighth-grade student with an OHI due to a heart condition, and she struggles with attendance. Which of the following would be the best example of a weekly objective in assisting Cheyenne in getting caught up?

a. Cheyenne will talk to each of her teachers at the beginning of each week.
b. Cheyenne will meet with her case manager to develop a plan for getting caught up.
c. Cheyenne will come in before school to talk to her teachers.
d. Cheyenne will complete all her missing assignments by the end of the week.

64. Dustin is a ninth-grade student who struggles with his organizational skills. Which of the following assistive technology devices would be most beneficial in helping him improve these skills?

a. FM listening systems
b. Speech recognition programs
c. Data managers
d. Abbreviation expanders

65. Which of the following is MOST likely to be a universally applicable lifelong writing skill for eighth-grade students?

a. Email writing
b. Essay writing
c. Letter writing
d. Résumé writing

66. Which of the following best describes how math simulation assistive technology can help students with disabilities access the curriculum?

a. Assisting students in recognizing the text
b. Assisting students in writing the problems
c. Assisting students in hearing the text
d. Assisting students in conceptualizing the problem

67. Which one of the following is the best example of cooperative learning when teaching a class that contains a mix of students with disabilities and the general education population?

a. Student-selected teams
b. Heterogeneous teams
c. Random teams
d. Homogeneous teams

68. Which of the following instructional strategies would be most appropriate when teaching a science lesson to a third-grade class?

a. Reciprocal teaching
b. Socratic questioning
c. Direct instruction
d. Learning centers

69. Which of the following instructional strategies would be most appropriate in supporting a student with an independent living skills goal of cooking a meal?

a. Allowing the student to help in the cafeteria by cleaning the kitchen
b. Allowing the student to shadow workers at a local restaurant
c. Allowing the student to research ingredients needed to make meals
d. Allowing the student to use the kitchen to cook her lunch each day

70. When co-teaching a high school English class, which one of the following instructional strategies is likely to be LEAST effective in ensuring that all students are achieving in the class?

a. Both teachers teaching as a team
b. Teaching the students in stations
c. One teacher instructing while the other supports
d. Teachers working together but without clearly defined objectives

71. When working with a group of students that struggle with study skills, which instructional strategy would be the MOST effective?

a. Group discussion
b. Independent practice
c. Portfolio development
d. Cooperative learning

72. The following teaching strategies all promote reading proficiency. Which one is more related to practice than to motivation?

a. Providing choices in the reading materials for students
b. Finding ways to make reading meaningful to students
c. Finding ways to make reading fun for students
d. Providing the students with many opportunities to read

73. Ms. Winslow has a class with many students with learning disabilities (LD). She consistently calls her students' attention to features in their textbooks such as boldface headings, illustrations, tables, charts, indexes, and chapter summaries. Which is most accurate regarding this practice?

a. Doing this helps her students to organize what they read and learn.
b. She does this because her students don't read textbooks.
c. It enhances her presentation but does not really facilitate learning.
d. This helps her LD students but is a waste of time for other students.

74. According to research findings, which of these is NOT a recommendation for improving the writing skills of students with learning disabilities?

a. Teaching students to set specific, attainable goals for writing
b. Teaching students strategies for planning, editing, and revising
c. Teaching students to avoid using writing for content learning
d. Teaching students how to use PC word processing programs

75. Jim has mild cognitive impairment. On annual standardized tests, his scores averaged 35% below national averages last year, compared to 20% below national averages this year. He scored 90% correct on his performance-based assessments. He has met or exceeded his IEP goals to increase his criterion-referenced classroom test scores by an average of 10% over the past year. Based on this information, which of the following is correct?

a. Jim's instruction is effective because he is demonstrating progress and meeting goals.
b. Jim's instruction is not effective enough because he scored well below national norms.
c. Jim's instruction is effective within the school but needs work for standardized tests.
d. Jim's instruction may or may not be effective; more information is needed to decide.

76. The type of assessment most often used to evaluate the effectiveness of instruction is a(n):

a. Authentic assessment
b. Ongoing assessment
c. Formative assessment
d. Summative assessment

77. One of the most important assessment tools for students with specific learning disabilities is a curriculum-based measure. Which of the following describes the MOST effective use of this kind of measure?

a. To determine whether or not a student is keeping up with his or her peers
b. To determine whether or not a student is making progress on his or her Individualized Education Program (IEP) goals
c. To determine whether or not a student is learning the curriculum
d. To determine whether or not a student has mastery of the curriculum

78. How can reading comprehension and vocabulary best be assessed?

a. They should be assessed with brief interviews and tests every two months to determine how much learning has taken place. Students learn in spurts, and in-depth assessments of comprehension and vocabulary are a waste of time.
b. They should be assessed by a rough combination of standardized testing, informal teacher observations, attention to grades, objective-linked assessments, and systematized charting of data over time.
c. They should be assessed by giving students weekly self-assessment rubrics to keep them constantly aware of and invested in their own progress.
d. They should be assessed by having students retell a story or summarize the content of an informational piece of writing. The degree to which the material was comprehended, and the richness or paucity of vocabulary used in such work, provides efficient and thorough assessment.

79. With each subject module, Ms. Lee assigns her students a series of projects. First, students might write a short essay about what they learned from a guest speaker's presentation. Then Ms. Lee might have them create a work of visual art—a drawing, painting, or collage—to represent some aspect of the subject. Later, she might give them a quiz on certain things they learned about the subject. She has given each student a place to keep all their project results—their essays, artworks, scored quizzes, and so forth. Each result is grouped by category or type. Periodically during the semester, Ms. Lee goes over these materials with each student individually. They review the progress they made from one essay to the next, one quiz to the next, one artwork to the next, etc. They then discuss the student's overall progress based on their review of all materials accumulated over time. The method Ms. Lee is using is:

a. An authentic assessment
b. A task analysis
c. A portfolio assessment
d. A performance assessment

80. Johnny's IQ score places him in the 97th percentile rank of the population. This means that:

a. 3 percent of the population has an IQ score higher than Johnny's.
b. 97 percent of the population has an IQ score higher than Johnny's.
c. 96 percent of the population has an IQ score higher than Johnny's.
d. 3 percent of the population has an IQ score lower than Johnny's.

81. In the table below are several test scores for the same individual student, Mario.

Z-SCORE	STANDARD SCORE	SCALED SCORE	T-SCORE	PERCENTILE
3.70	155	20	87	99.99

Based on this table, which of the following is correct?

a. These must be scores Mario got on several different tests.
b. Mario scored much higher in some areas of a test than others.
c. If these are IQ scores, Mario must be a gifted student.
d. If these are IQ scores, Mario must have intellectual disabilities.

82. Andrea is a first-grade student with a developmental delay. Which formative assessment can be implemented to best monitor her progress throughout the school year?

a. Interviewing her each week
b. Giving her academic probes
c. Observing her in class
d. Monitoring her test scores

83. How can a summative assessment be implemented for students with disabilities?

a. Monitoring their progress on IEP goals
b. Asking them to complete a portfolio at the end of a unit
c. Evaluating them for continued eligibility
d. Diagnosing which accommodations they need

84. Jacob is a third-grade student who scored one standard deviation below average in written expression on an academic achievement test. Which of the following best describes the likely next step for Jacob?

a. Jacob will be determined eligible for special education services.
b. Jacob will need additional tests specific to written expression.
c. Jacob will need to be administered an intelligence test.
d. Jacob will need to be evaluated for special education services.

85. Shamus is an eighth-grade student with a specific learning disability in the area of written expression. Which of the following is the best example of a curriculum-based measure to monitor his progress in this area?

a. Giving him a story starter and counting his correct writing sequences
b. Giving him a list of spelling words to memorize and spell
c. Giving him a class period to construct an essay
d. Giving him a picture and asking him to write a sentence

86. Ricky is a seventh-grade student being evaluated for special education services who is administered an IQ test. Which of the following best describes the results of his test if he scored a 100?

a. Ricky scored in the average range.
b. Ricky got all the questions correct.
c. Ricky does not need special education services.
d. Ricky does need special education services.

87. Which of the following best describes the purpose of state standardized tests?

a. To compare a student's academic achievement to a norm
b. To determine how much progress a student has made
c. To find strengths and weaknesses in a student's development
d. To determine the intellectual ability of students

88. Which of the following best describes when it would be necessary for a teacher to create their own assessment?

a. When students do not have access to the curriculum
b. When testing students with intellectual disabilities
c. When providing accommodations to students
d. When the academic standards are modified

89. Matthew is a third-grade student with an emotional disturbance who struggles with outbursts. Which of the following observation methods would be most beneficial when conducting a formative assessment?

a. Tally marks
b. Time sampling
c. Qualitative observations
d. Verbatim scripting

90. When interpreting the results of a norm-referenced test, how are the scores determined?

a. By comparing a student's score to a previous score
b. By comparing a student's score to other students that are the same age
c. By comparing a student's score to a standard deviation
d. By comparing a student's score to other students with disabilities

91. Which of the following describes the purpose of an intelligence test?

a. To measure a student's ability to think abstractly
b. To measure a student's ability to understand spoken language
c. To measure a student's ability to convey ideas through oral language
d. To measure a student's ability to retain visual information

92. Peyton is a new student at Harbor Light High School. He is a ninth-grade student with a specific learning disability in the area of math problem solving. How can a diagnostic assessment be used to best guide his math instruction?

a. Assessing which accommodations he can access
b. Assessing which math class is most appropriate
c. Assessing which goals to develop in his IEP
d. Assessing which modifications need to be made

93. Christopher is a student with concerns in the area of academics who scored in the below-average range on an academic achievement test. Which of the following disability categories would Christopher most likely be eligible for?

a. Speech or language impairment
b. Other health impairment
c. Specific learning disability
d. Cognitive disability

94. Which of the following would NOT be an example of a diagnostic assessment?

a. Pretests
b. Self-assessments
c. Interviews
d. Projects

95. Lisa is a fifth-grade student with a disability who will often exhibit defiance in her class. Which of the following would be the best example of a formative assessment in order to evaluate Lisa's behavior?

a. Asking her to participate in class discussions
b. Conferring with her throughout the year
c. Observing her behavior in the class
d. Allowing her to skip certain lessons

96. Corey is a third-grade student with a specific learning disability in the area of reading fluency. Which of the following assessments would be most appropriate in determining his eligibility for special education services?

a. Wechsler Preschool and Primary Scale of Intelligence
b. Wechsler Individual Achievement Test
c. Wechsler Intelligence Scale
d. Wechsler Intelligence Scale for Children

97. Which of the following statements is true of professional development?

a. Professional development is not site-specific, since some principles of teaching are universal.
b. Professional development is about strategies rather than content.
c. Professional development is not necessarily job-embedded, because it is an opportunity to explore other educational roles.
d. Professional development is designed by experts and teachers.

98. Laws and ethics are important areas of concern for the classroom teacher, starting with an understanding of the differences between laws and ethics. Of the following statements, which one is FALSE?

a. Laws are concrete, written, and enacted by people.
b. Ethics are less tangible and observable and consist of ideas.
c. Laws are always ethical.
d. Most laws are the codification of what society considers moral or ethical obligations.

99. Aaron, a student in Mr. Love's class, has a diagnosis of attention-deficit/hyperactivity disorder. Aaron's mother has a history of some difficulties with compliance in giving Aaron his daily medication. Today Aaron does not remain on task for more than a few seconds at a time, and he does not stay in his seat for more than five minutes at a time. This is not typical of his daily behavior in the classroom. What should Mr. Love do?

a. Contact Aaron's doctor and recommend that his medication be reevaluated for a higher dose.
b. Contact Aaron's mother and ask whether she was able to give him his medication today.
c. Contact the school principal and recommend that Aaron be placed in a different classroom.
d. Contact Aaron's doctor and recommend that he be reevaluated for a different medication.

100. When a student's behavior warrants alternative placement, how should the school determine appropriate placement?

a. Contact the student's parents and have them decide what is best for the student.
b. Talk to the student and let him or her choose the best placement.
c. Convene the placement review committee.
d. Suspend the student during an investigation.

101. Which of the following pieces of information is typically NOT required during the prereferral process for special education?

a. Parental consent
b. Data
c. Monitoring
d. Strategy discussion

102. For an incoming student from a different culture, which of the following characteristics has the greatest impact on the identification of special education needs?

a. The language the student speaks
b. The content the student has learned
c. The location the student comes from
d. The religion the student practices

103. Which of the following is correct regarding the IEP process?

a. A student's educational/behavioral difficulties will be documented and explained during prereferral.
b. The effectiveness of classroom accommodations and modifications are tested after eligibility determination.
c. Different instructional interventions will be assessed for effectiveness after the IEP is implemented.
d. The student's progress will be monitored only after the IEP has been developed and implemented.

104. Sandra is a special education teacher. At the facility where she works, which serves many students with multiple physical disabilities, the occupational therapist schedules regular OT clinics. Of the staff at this facility, who should attend these OT clinics?

a. The OT who plans the clinic, other OTs and OT aides, and the physical therapist
b. The OT staff, the direct care workers, the nurse, and the physical therapist
c. The OT staff, the doctor, and the nurses
d. The OT staff, PT staff, nurses, teachers, activity therapist, direct care workers, and behavior specialist

105. Mr. Campbell has several students in his class whose families are of lower socioeconomic status (SES). These students have been getting consistently lower grades and standardized test scores than the class average. These students are then transferred to Mr. Leon's class. Mr. Leon grew up with lower SES himself. In their new class, these students are getting grades and standardized test scores equal to the class average. What is the most likely reason for this?

a. Mr. Leon is biased in favor of these students because they have similar backgrounds.
b. Mr. Campbell was biased against these students out of a prevalent middle-class bias.
c. The students feel more comfortable in Mr. Leon's class, increasing their motivation.
d. The students were uncomfortable in Mr. Campbell's class and were underachieving.

106. Joel lived for many years at an institution and has now been placed in a group home. He has profound intellectual disabilities and a number of obsessive-compulsive behaviors. He has certain habits; for example, at meals he tends to sit sideways at the table with his legs crossed, with the result that he drops a great deal of food on the floor. What should the houseparent do?

a. Put Joel in a time-out for the rest of the meal when this occurs.
b. Direct Joel to clean up the floor after the meal is over.
c. Meet with Joel's IEP team to write training objectives.
d. Place a drop cloth on the floor under Joel's chair.

107. Pam has mild intellectual disabilities and autism. She has lived in more than one group home placement. She is a model student and helps all her housemates in the group home. She gets dressed first and gets all of their lunches out of the refrigerator before they leave for school. She helps the houseparents by setting and clearing the table at dinnertime, and she also helps clean the house. Pam has been recommended for a new program in which she will work part-time in supported employment, take classes part-time, and will live in a more independent group home with supervision. Rather than constant shifts of houseparents, in this program there are onsite, part-time supervisors who are also available around the clock when they are offsite. If paged or phoned they will come immediately to the home as needed. Pam seems very interested in this program. Her parents, however, are nervous about it. They are very protective. What should be done here?

a. Pam should not enter this program as it makes her parents too uncomfortable.
b. Pam should enter this program regardless of her parents' fears.
c. Pam and her parents should meet first with program staff and former staff.
d. Pam should move into the new home on a trial basis to see how it works out.

108. Of the following criteria for defining intellectual disabilities, which one was widely used only from 1961 on?

a. Mental deficiency/incomplete development
b. Originates during the developmental period
c. Associated with impaired adaptive behavior
d. A condition manifested at maturity

109. Which of the following is a disadvantage of an externally facilitated IEP meeting?

a. The discussion can often get off topic.
b. It can be difficult to resolve conflicts.
c. It can make certain members feel left out.
d. It takes more time to prepare.

110. Tran is a student who recently arrived in the US from Vietnam. According to federal regulations mandated by the Individuals with Disabilities Education Act, which can be done if a learning disability is suspected?

a. Give Tran an IQ test to determine whether he has any specific learning disability.
b. Give Tran a reading evaluation test and a writing evaluation test, both in English.
c. Give Tran special education, depending on tests, with written parental consent.
d. Give Tran a written IEP for a learning disability regardless of the results of tests.

111. Kim is in a general education classroom and receives special education sessions for a mild disability. She wants to talk to her special education teacher about her college applications. Which of the following is the correct scenario for such a conversation?

a. They discuss the subject in the hallway with students, faculty, and staff passing by.
b. They discuss the subject in the teacher's office during a small group therapy session.
c. They discuss the subject alone together in the teacher's office during a free period.
d. They discuss the subject in Kim's general education classroom before class begins.

112. Greg is a student with intellectual disabilities who qualified for group home placement in the community and has been living there successfully for a while. His late mother provided his personal care when he was growing up. Greg has a poor sense of balance and recently slipped in the shower, fell, and broke his hip. His father still approves of the placement but is currently very anxious about his son being injured again. What might be appropriate for his teacher to do?

a. Recommend a different placement with more direct personal care to avoid more falls.
b. Counsel Greg's father that the injury was unfortunate but that these things happen in life.
c. Initiate an investigation of the group home staff to determine if they were negligent.
d. Work with residential services on installing nonslip flooring and grab bars in the tub.

113. Stewart is a student who uses a wheelchair. This year he will be placed in Ms. Joplin's class, where all the other students are ambulatory. He will be the only student in a wheelchair. Stewart's IEP team is meeting to discuss his placement. Regarding concerns about the wheelchair, what is the best recommendation?

a. Stewart should not be placed in this class, because his wheelchair will stand out, making both him and the other students feel uncomfortable about it.
b. Someone should accompany Stewart to transfer him from his wheelchair to a regular student desk/chair and then back to his wheelchair when it is time to leave the classroom.
c. Stewart should only be placed in a class that has other students who use wheelchairs.
d. School staff should ensure that the classroom is wheelchair-accessible and that Stewart can navigate it; they should also show other students how to adjust to the situation.

114. Which of the following best describes the purpose of the Education for All Handicapped Children Act of 1975?

a. To mandate free appropriate public education for students with disabilities
b. To provide grants to states to fund special education programs
c. To establish services to facilitate school-to-work transitions
d. To allow students with disabilities to be included in statewide assessments

115. Javier is a fourth-grade student with an emotional disturbance. Which one of the following individuals is LEAST likely to attend IEP meetings?

a. School psychologist
b. Director of special education
c. The student
d. School principal

116. Which of the following is NOT one of the dispute-resolution processes that a parent or stakeholder may choose for a child with a disability who receives special education services?

a. Filing a complaint with the Department of Education
b. Asking to find a compromise through mediation
c. Filing a due process complaint
d. Removing the student from the school

117. Which of the following is true about the Family Educational Rights and Privacy Act and students with disabilities?

a. Each teacher in the school has access to the student's IEP.
b. Schools are not required to allow parents to inspect previous IEPs.
c. Previous IEPs can be amended at any time.
d. Parents have the right to access testing protocols.

118. Which of the following is LEAST likely to be the responsibility of an elementary school special education teacher?

a. Communicating accommodations to general education teachers
b. Managing the schedules of paraprofessionals
c. Team-teaching lessons in the classroom setting
d. Facilitating 504 plans and meetings

119. Madison is a third-grade student who receives special education services due to a hearing impairment. Which of the following special service providers would be LEAST likely to attend her reevaluation meeting?

a. Speech-language pathologist
b. Occupational therapist
c. School nurse
d. District audiologist

120. Which of the following best describes the primary role during MTSS problem-solving meetings when a special education evaluation is being considered?

a. To provide input on students with disabilities
b. To discuss students who may need to be evaluated
c. To provide interventions for students
d. To discuss students who exit special education

Answer Key and Explanations for Test #2

1. D: Antecedents are events that occur right before a problem behavior and can trigger the behavior. Consequences are events that occur right after a problem behavior and can reinforce the behavior. The ABC model of behavior analysis examines the sequence of an antecedent occurring, which then triggers the behavior, which is then reinforced by the consequence following the behavior. Knowing what precipitates the behavior, and what rewards it, helps to determine the behavior's function, or what it accomplishes for the individual.

2. D: Dysgraphia. Dysgraphic individuals cannot manage the physical act of writing. While many dysgraphics are highly intelligent and able to express themselves cogently, they have extreme difficulty holding a writing implement and shaping letters.

3. C: Gardner's multiple-intelligences framework includes verbal-linguistic, logical-mathematical, musical, visual-spatial, bodily-kinesthetic, interpersonal, intrapersonal, naturalistic, and existential intelligences. Teachers can use this framework to vary instruction and provide multiple ways for students, including students with learning disabilities, to engage with content.

4. D: He goes out of his way to annoy others, is defiant, and goes into childish rages in which he blames others. This student has been diagnosed with oppositional defiant disorder, a psychiatric disorder characterized by noncompliance, tantrums, extremely irritating conduct, refusal to follow rules, argumentative behavior, and blaming others.

5. D: With cerebral palsy, the degree of disability can vary widely among individuals, so option A is incorrect.

A diagnosis of intellectual disabilities does not necessarily mean a student will have greater or lesser special education needs than those with only cerebral palsy. Their needs will depend on their individual abilities. For example, some students with cerebral palsy may have greater physical disabilities than some other students with both cerebral palsy and intellectual disabilities, so option B is incorrect.

While a student with mild intellectual disabilities may have a very different educational plan than a student with severe or profound disabilities, this does not necessarily mean that the lower-functioning students need a greater amount of intervention. They may have different assignments, different presentation modalities, and varying levels of difficulty, but they will not necessarily require more time or attention than higher-functioning intellectually disabled students. The level of severity is only one of many factors. For example, a student with mild intellectual disabilities and a higher IQ score could have more profound physical disabilities from CP than another student and thus require more adaptive devices and physical assistance, so option C is incorrect.

Since the degree of disability can vary widely among individuals with cerebral palsy and since the same is true of individuals with intellectual disabilities, option D is correct.

6. B: A deficit in receptive communication is reflected by difficulty understanding the spoken language that one hears. Deficits in expressive communication (A) are reflected in difficulties with speaking. This may be related to language processing (as in difficulty retrieving words or constructing sentences) or speech (as in poor articulation, stuttering, or voice problems). Verbal communication (C) refers to using words vs. nonverbal communication such as gestures, body language, and facial expression, but this term does not differentiate between expressive and receptive communication. Social communication (D) is communication used in social interactions, but understanding spoken language is not limited to social interactions (it also occurs in classes, lectures, audio/video recordings, etc.).

7. C: The child may or may not be hyperactive, but the fact that she can control her behavior for extended periods if a reward is involved suggests the child is overly indulged outside of class. In addition, she appears to act out in an effort to seek peer admiration; this excludes the possibility of Tourette syndrome and attention-deficit/hyperactivity disorder. In the first case, she would be unlikely to seek approval. In the second, she would be unlikely to be able to control herself under certain circumstances. There is nothing in her behavior to suggest psychosis.

8. A: Students with ADHD are most likely to also have a learning disability compared to students without ADHD. ADHD can affect attention, focus, executive functioning, which may contribute to difficulties in reading, math, or written expression. While students with ADHD may experience speech impairments, depression, or anxiety, these co-occurring conditions are less frequent than learning disabilities. Therefore, answers B, C, and D are incorrect.

9. A: James can grasp an object inserted into his fist, so he could point to various pictures on a communication board with a pointer to communicate his needs. Therefore, option A is correct.

A computer with keyboard would not help James. He does not have the manual ability to type due to his contractures. He is also illiterate. Therefore, option B is incorrect.

A voice-activated computer would not do any good as James cannot speak. Therefore, option C is incorrect.

An adaptive holder for manipulating a pen would not work for James, as he could not use it due to the severe contractures of his hands, and he cannot read or write. Therefore, option D is incorrect.

10. B: A computer with a built-in voice synthesizer would let Stephen program all the words in his vocabulary into it. He could express himself despite his paralyzed vocal cords. He has excellent expressive and receptive language skills and a high IQ, so this would be the best solution for him. Therefore, option B is correct.

Adaptive pencil and paper holders would not help Stephen, because he can only press buttons with one hand. He could not manipulate a writing implement due to his paralysis. Therefore, option A is incorrect.

An electrolarynx is used by some laryngectomy patients whose larynxes have been surgically removed because of laryngeal cancer. It is an alternative to learning esophageal speech. This device is handheld. Stephen could not hold it up to his throat as required. The device also requires the speech system's muscles to work. It emits a tone, and the user manipulates the tongue, lips, cheeks, and throat, as in normal speech, to modulate the tone into recognizable speech sounds. Stephen could not use this device due to his paralysis. Therefore, option C is incorrect.

A communication board with buttons would be a good option for a student who is younger or less intellectually gifted than Stephen. It would afford simpler communication of basic needs and feelings. With Stephen's high IQ and advanced academic skills, he can program a computer with more complex ideas and complete sentences. He would undoubtedly find the communication board limited and would be frustrated. Therefore, option D is incorrect.

11. B: Now that Jan is used to hearing the alarm, it has helped her become aware that she has urinated. The next step is for her to become aware that she is wet without needing the alarm to alert her. Raising her hand and vocalizing is a way she can communicate to staff that she knows this. Therefore, option B is correct.

Having Jan try to control her bladder at this stage is skipping too many steps for an individual with intellectual disabilities. She is being alerted by the sound of the alarm. She needs many more steps before she gets to the point of controlling her bladder. Therefore, option A is incorrect.

Vocalizing when she hears the alarm is not necessary since staff can hear the alarm. It is also not a step forward. Once the alarm has made Jan aware that she has urinated, the next step is for her to become aware of this without needing the alarm. She still wears the alarm as a transitional device to help remind her to signal when she feels wet. It can be phased out eventually, once she is able to notice being wet without waiting to hear the sound. Therefore, option C is incorrect.

Wheeling herself to the bathroom would be the step after the step of controlling her bladder (option A), so Jan is not ready for this step yet. This will be the final step in the training process. She will need to be able to control her bladder first, and she is not even at that step yet. Therefore, option D is incorrect.

12. D: Environmental factors that lead to positive development include the influences from the outside world that shape who we are or who we become. Having intelligent parents is a biological factor that may shape who we are. Answers A, B, and C are incorrect because each of these involve environmental factors and influences that come from the outside world. Although they may each have a positive impact, they would be considered environmental factors.

13. B: A class may not be available. If one were available, it might teach useful skills but it would not be the same as gaining real-life experience. Also, William will be attending college classes and working part-time, so enrolling in another class on top of these commitments could overload his schedule. Therefore option A is incorrect.

Since William is proficient with computers, referring him to a website is a natural choice. The TASH website, for example, has a link to its Bridge Network, a free resource network that provides access to a database of contact information incorporating many needs of persons with disabilities. It includes resources for transitions from school to adult life, self-determination, and community living, among many others. Telling William about a website like this would enable him to locate resources on his own and avail himself of the support he needs to make this transition. Therefore option B is correct.

Advising William to try living on his own with a roommate with no previous such experience would provide him with no transition. Being autistic and spending a lot of time with computers, William may not have the best social skills for living with a roommate. Since he is interested in doing this but feels unsure how to go about it, he should not just attempt it without any preparation. He is less likely to experience success that way. Therefore option C is incorrect.

William could feasibly choose to stay at home while he attends classes and works. In many ways it would be easier than making a change. However, since he is interested in independent living, continuing to live at home would be a lack of progress. It would be better to encourage him to pursue his interest in progress and offer him sources of support and information to accomplish his objective. Therefore option D is incorrect.

14. A: Students from impoverished urban settings often have no experience with a cup and saucer as a set that go together; they may never have seen these two objects together in real life. It would be logical to them that a cup goes on the table. This example demonstrates the cultural bias of many standardized tests. Therefore, option A is correct.

Whereas some children may suffer from cognitive impairment if they have been malnourished, this is not true of all children from poor urban families. When a lack of familiarity with certain cultural customs influences their choice, as in this cup and saucer example, it would be erroneous to assume instead that their language development is delayed without other objective proof of this. Therefore, option B is incorrect.

While there is a correlation between poverty and lower educational levels, it is not true that all people of lower income lack critical thinking skills or do not teach these skills to their children. There are many other factors contributing to a complex issue such as urban poverty. Therefore, option C is incorrect.

It is not true that children living in poverty never read books at home. There are many families who have little financially or materially, but who are literate and even love to read. (Consider the childhoods of famous people like Abraham Lincoln, Frederick Douglass, or Oprah Winfrey. They were all extremely poor growing up and all loved to read.) Therefore, option D is incorrect.

15. C: It is very common for children with ADHD to also exhibit a learning disability in one or more areas. These students will often struggle to attend to their education, which causes them to fall behind and struggle with their learning. It is important to recognize and understand which disabilities a student may struggle with. Answer A is incorrect because learning disabilities are the most common co-occurring conditions with ADHD. Answer B is incorrect because speech problems tend to be more common in students with ADHD. Answer D is incorrect because fewer than half of students with ADHD also have conduct disorders.

16. D: The humanism theory suggests that humans are innately good and have a need to make themselves better. The theory states that human experiences influence peoples' behaviors and decisions, but it takes an optimistic approach to the human experience. Although the theory states that each person is inherently good, it does not define what this means or how it is measured. Answer A is incorrect because a lack of internal influences is a criticism of the behaviorism learning theory. Answer B is incorrect because not considering the social aspect of learning is a common criticism of the cognitivism theory. Answer C is incorrect because being relative and not providing right or wrong answers are elements of the constructivism theory.

17. B: Students who are English learners do not necessarily exhibit a learning disability in their native language before English. Sometimes the deficit is apparent in one language and not the other, and many times it is apparent in both. It is important to understand the history of each student when making the determination. Answer A is incorrect because there is not one single test that predicts special education eligibility for English learners. Answer C is incorrect because it is imperative that these students receive proper learning before they can be properly evaluated. Answer D is incorrect because where a student was raised and what they know can also be deciding factors.

18. C: Although all of these choices may impact students throughout their lifetimes, students with multiple disabilities are likely to be impacted the most. Students with multiple disabilities have two or more disabilities that severely impact their access to education. One of these disabilities is typically an intellectual disability, which impacts students throughout their life. Answer A is incorrect because developmental delays typically impact younger students and may or may not last throughout a person's lifetime. Answer B is incorrect because students that have just speech or language impairments may end up learning to overcome these disabilities eventually. Answer D is incorrect because although specific learning disabilities may impact students in different ways, these are less likely to have an impact on a person than someone with multiple disabilities.

19. A: One of the typical emotional developments of a preschool student is playing games with friends or others. Children of this age will often start to change the rules of a game or make up their own rules to make it more fun or interesting. Recognizing the emotions of students during these social interactions is important in determining whether or not they are developing at the expected rate. Answer B is incorrect because being overly rigid and not wanting to change their routine or schedule is not usually considered typical of a preschool student. Answer C is incorrect because preschool students typically start to be less dependent on their caregivers during this time. While some issues with turn-taking may still be present in this age group, answer D is incorrect because children most often develop the ability to take turns without significant issues before entering preschool.

20. D: Although all of these factors can have an enormous impact on a person and everyone may be impacted in a different way, the support system is typically the most beneficial. Without a support system in place, which may include parents, siblings, or other friends or family members, it will be difficult for individuals with disabilities to follow their own path to making a positive impact on society. Research shows that individuals with disabilities are more likely to succeed when they have a positive support system. Answer A is incorrect because although the type of disability is certainly impactful, individuals with all kinds of disabilities can succeed with proper support. Answer B is incorrect because the personality is important, but it does not have as much of an impact as a support system in place. Answer C is incorrect because the meaning of the disability may or may not be impactful for some individuals.

21. C: Positive behavioral interventions are more effective when they teach a more appropriate behavior to replace the problem behavior. Because all behaviors have some function, a problem behavior cannot simply be eliminated; some other behavior will arise to fulfill the same purpose. Interventions to control problem behaviors (A) or to suppress them (B) are not considered positive. These tend not to be maintained over time or generalized to other situations as there is no positive replacement for the undesirable behavior. It is not the interventions that analyze the behavior (D) but the prior analysis on which the subsequent intervention is based.

22. B: The COACH model (Giangreco, Cloninger, and Iverson 1998) is a collaborative approach described by educational researchers as "student-directed planning," which they claim goes "beyond person-centered planning" (Wehmeyer et al. 2002) by making the student central in the process. Person-centered planning typically centers more on family and social support systems. GAP (Turnbull & Turnbull 2002) (A); MAPs (Pearpoint, Forest, and O'Brien 1996) (C); and PATH (D), which extends the MAPs process to develop "a more definitive plan of action," are all examples of person-centered planning.

23. D: Enthusiastically accepted. The adults discuss a background check and the possibility the teen might discover gardening is not for her and want to quit. However, this is most likely to occur early in her employment, giving the neighbor sufficient time to find another helper. The teacher is pleased because the girl will learn new skills through modeling and repetition. The mother is pleased because the experience will add to the girl's self-esteem and show her she is capable of learning. The elderly neighbor is pleased because she is both compassionate and truly needs help. The girl is delighted the neighbor recognizes her potential and sees her as valuable.

24. C: Until the teacher monitors the child's verbal abilities and habits, she cannot determine if the lack of interaction suggests a learning disability, an emotional problem, or simply a shy personality. The teacher should informally observe the child over a period of time, noting if and when she initiates or responds to oral language, if she is reading with apparent comprehension, if her vocabulary is limited, and the degree to which the child is interested in understanding.

25. B: A teacher's expectations are the desired result of their goals. On the other hand, goals are the means to obtaining the outcomes. For example, a goal may be to complete lesson one by the end of week one. This goal will determine the activities the teacher plans for that week. The teacher will also have the expectation that her student will complete and understand the lesson. Rules and procedures typically refer to acceptable behavior in the classroom. Effective classroom management will detail the rules of the classroom as well as the process to follow those rules. Taken together, well-thought-out goals, expectations, rules, and procedures will yield a well-run classroom.

26. B: Constructive assertiveness is used when a teacher is able to identify a problem, state their concerns in a clear and concise manner, and strive to correct the behaviors as soon as possible. Using these methods, the teacher does not make a direct attack on the student. Instead, the teacher works with the student to correct problems. However, teachers must be cautious, because assertiveness is a continuum, which can range from hostile to constructive. The words a teacher uses, as well as their body language, will send signals to the students and determine their response to the teacher.

27. C: There should be follow-up to the conflict resolution to ensure that the children are sticking to their agreed-upon solution and that the conflict does not reoccur. Some teachers might feel that dropping the issue will help everyone forget the conflict, but that usually is not the case. Conflicts are best handled with calmness and a quiet voice as the teacher gathers information about the conflict in order to get a complete and fair picture of the situation. Then the teacher should review the conflict with the children and ask for their input about ways the problem could have been prevented and ways to solve the conflict. Involving the children in the resolution of the problem teaches them self-regulation and respect for themselves and others.

28. A: While all of these strategies could be helpful, maintaining consistency in the schedule is the foundational strategy for supporting students who have difficulty coping with change. When visitors or special events do occur, it helps, of course, to prepare the students by telling them in advance of the change in schedule. Those children who are still disturbed by the change can be helped by being near someone they trust during the visit or activity. The teacher can even teach relaxation techniques to the students and suggest these techniques when a student appears to be having anxiety over a change in routine, but these strategies are secondary to maintaining the schedule as much as possible.

29. B: Although all these choices may be helpful for Jimmy, it would be most appropriate for Jimmy's teachers to attempt some accommodations in the classroom. The first step in the prereferral process for special education is to provide additional supports for students inside the general education classroom. If this support is unsuccessful, then it may be a good idea to seek additional support and refer to the special education team. Answer A is incorrect because it is important to attempt interventions to determine how a student would respond before referring to special education. Answer C is incorrect because although a tutor may be helpful for Jimmy, it is best to first try some accommodations to see if those are successful. Answer D is incorrect because it may not be appropriate to offer to work with Jimmy after school.

30. D: Restraints should not be used except in extreme cases to prevent injury to oneself or others. Richard's behaviors do not harm anybody. Research shows that restraining movements does not eventually stop them. Therefore, option A is incorrect.

Noise-making instruments would provide auditory stimuli for Richard but would be disruptive to others. Additionally, this option would only serve as a replacement for the self-stimulatory behavior and would not serve to further enrich his learning environment. Therefore, option B is incorrect.

Head weaving is common in blind individuals. It is often a means of getting sensory feedback in the absence of visual stimuli and can also provide proprioceptive and kinesthetic orientation. Regardless, Richard will have a neurological assessment as part of his physician's examination, but there is no special indication to look for problems on account of head weaving. This behavior can be normal in some blind individuals. Therefore, option C is incorrect.

Because he is blind and has profound intellectual disabilities, a program of sensory stimulation using his other senses would benefit Richard as it would enrich his environment and enhance his learning ability. A need for additional sensory stimulation may also be indicated by Richard's hand clapping. Therefore, option D is correct.

31. D: Books in large print and on teen-related topics but with simplified text are the ideal combination for Clyde's visual impairment, age, and reading comprehension level. Therefore, option D is correct.

Large-print books are a good idea for Clyde's visual impairment, and subjects relevant to teens are appropriate for his age, but not for his first-grade reading level. Therefore, option A is incorrect.

Children's books have the large print and simple subject matter Clyde needs, but they are not appropriate for his age. Therefore, option B is incorrect.

With the availability of large-print textbooks, a magnifying glass is not the easiest way for Clyde to read. Having one would certainly expand the types of media he could see, and it would be beneficial for him to have it if he should want or need to see the small print in everyday media like newspapers and phone books. But for reading, it would not be as easy on his eyes as large print. Also, many books with regular-size print will be beyond Clyde's first-grade level of reading comprehension. Therefore, option C is incorrect.

32. A: The first option includes activities in three different settings: school, home/family, and community, and all three activities are focused on conversations, which represent one aspect of social interaction. This is a good example of incorporating social skills instruction across settings. It also addresses these particular students' needs, so option A is correct.

The second option includes only two settings—the classroom and a field trip. The in-class activities are reading and writing about social skills but do not include any direct practice of these skills. It is not clear whether the field trip and the essay about the trip included any learning or practice of social skills, so option B is incorrect.

All the activities in the third option take place in community settings, with no activities occurring in school or at home. There is no balance of settings in this scenario as there is in the first option. While taking turns, orderly behavior, and following instructions can be types of social skills, these are not areas in which these students need work, so option C is incorrect.

All the activities in the last option take place in the home, with none occurring in the school or community. The activities also do not include any practice in needed social skills. They include only written homework, keeping a record of family interactions, and watching an educational TV program with their families. These do not involve initiating interactions, using appropriate behaviors during interactions, or participating more fully in social activities, which are the skills these students need, so option D is incorrect.

33. B: The first step is to determine what function(s) or purpose(s) the behaviors serve by conducting a functional behavior analysis (FBA). Students are not usually referred for special education without first trying classroom interventions determined through an FBA; also, a conduct or behavior disorder should not be assumed if it has not been diagnosed after thorough evaluation (A). Moving the student to a separate classroom (C) is also inappropriate. Even after the FBA, classroom interventions, referral if indicated, evaluation, diagnosis, and placement in special education if indicated, the least restrictive environment as dictated by law is more likely to be inclusive than segregated. Recommending special school placement to parents (D) is also premature and inappropriate.

34. C: When maintaining a skill, it is important to practice that skill periodically over the course of time. For someone that struggles with reading comprehension, it is important to practice reading multiple times to ensure that the content is remembered. Students with disabilities who struggle in certain areas will likely need extra practice for maintaining these skills. Answer A is incorrect because simply reading the story a few times in a row will not allow the student to maintain the skill long-term. Answer B is incorrect because just rereading the story once for homework likely will not allow him to maintain the skill either. Answer D is incorrect because although quizzing himself may be a valuable strategy in helping him remember the story, it likely will not allow him to maintain this skill.

35. A: Although all of these choices may be beneficial to students with disabilities, a functional curriculum is designed to teach students independent living skills. This curriculum typically replaces traditional secondary curriculum for certain students who may be candidates at the high school level. It tends to be designed for students who will struggle to live independently once they complete their schooling. Answer B is incorrect because although it may be helpful in developing communication skills, the sole purpose is not just for this communication development. Answer C is incorrect because functional curriculum is an alternative curriculum rather than teaching the basic subjects. Answer D is incorrect because the primary goal of functional curriculum is to teach independent living skills, not just to teach current everyday tasks.

36. A: The behaviorist learning theory states that the teacher teaches correct behaviors and the students understand them and apply them in the classroom. According to this theory, students learn these behaviors via positive and negative reinforcement. This is important in understanding which techniques and learning theories might be best for certain students as they learn. Answer B is incorrect because the behaviorist theory states that the student is shaped through reinforcement rather than self-learning. Answer C is incorrect because the teacher facilitating collaborative groups is an example of the constructivist learning theory. Answer D is incorrect because the teacher guiding students in understanding the environment is an example of the cognitivism theory.

37. C: Offering the corner workspace to reward good behavior, such as active participation in class, is the best way to use a corner workspace. Teachers should be very consistent with implementation of incentives, as reinforcement can backfire if a reward is used incorrectly. Chad usually requires active involvement from the teacher to stay on task, so giving Chad extra space to do work is not likely to be a successful solution. It is important to have a consistent plan for the corner to only be used when Chad is finished with his assignments for the day. Since Chad likely perceives the corner workspace as a reward, it is not a good idea to use it when Chad is disruptive, as it may help to reinforce disruptive behaviors. Similarly, Chad should not be allowed to use the corner whenever he thinks he needs a break, as Chad may try to take advantage of the incentive to avoid doing work.

38. C: Students in fourth grade typically do not display frequent lying and dishonesty. Although they may tell small lies from time to time, it is concerning if lying becomes a pattern for a child of this age. It is important to recognize these kinds of patterns when observing students in order to determine the cause and potentially seek help if necessary. Answer A is incorrect because fourth graders may start to experiment with swear words. Answer B is incorrect because bragging is also considered a normal behavior for a fourth-grade student who is seeking attention. Answer D is incorrect because having disagreements is something that would be considered typical for a fourth grader.

39. D: Changing the environment in which a student is taught does not typically provide a student access to the general education curriculum. If special education students are taught outside the general education setting in a special education classroom, they do not have the same access to the content and to their peers. It is important to provide this access to students as much as possible. Answer A is incorrect because changing the content to meet their needs still provides them access to the same curriculum. Answer B is incorrect because changing the method in which they are taught also provides the same curriculum with a different method. Answer C is incorrect because changing how they demonstrate knowledge is also allowing students to access the general education curriculum in a way that meets their needs.

40. B: Although sharing control over the classroom may sometimes be a positive, many teachers may struggle to work together to make co-teaching successful. Unless the roles and responsibilities of each teacher are clearly defined, it may be difficult for each teacher to share control of the classroom. It may also be difficult to find time to plan lessons together, which could potentially make it a struggle to have a shared vision. Therefore, sharing control of the classroom does not accurately describe the purpose of the co-teaching model. Answer A is incorrect because co-teaching can increase the amount of attention that students receive because there are multiple teachers in the class. Answer C is incorrect because differentiation should be increased in the co-teaching model because one of the teachers in the class is focused on the struggling learners. Answer D is incorrect because typically in the co-teaching model one of the teachers is an expert in the subject area and the other is a special education teacher.

41. A: Although small-group pull-outs can provide opportunities for all of these choices, allowing these students to access their IEP accommodations is most important. These accommodations may include a quiet setting to learn, having texts read to them, or being retaught certain concepts. At the high school level, it is important to provide these accommodations to students so they can access as much of the general education curriculum as possible. Answer B is incorrect because students should be allowed to ask questions in any instructional setting, not just pull-outs. Answer C is incorrect because reducing teacher workload is not an instructional benefit. The purpose of separation is to improve student learning, not solely to make teaching easier. Answer D is incorrect because extra practice in reading, writing, or math is a secondary benefit. It may happen, but only if it aligns with the IEP goals.

42. B: The use of consequences would be considered a negative behavior intervention because it is a reaction to a student's poor behavior. Positive behavior interventions typically include strategies for the student to use when they might be experiencing frustration. These tend to be strategies for the student or teacher to use before the event takes place, rather than after. Answer A is incorrect because social-emotional strategies can be beneficial in helping the student to stay calm in certain situations. Answer C is incorrect because self-regulatory strategies can also help a student avoid negative behavior. Answer D is incorrect because coping skills are valuable in handling stress.

43. D: Although all of these choices may be beneficial for students with autism, providing hands-on instruction would likely be the best option. It is important to provide different options for students to learn, especially those students who may struggle with the content. Giving students an opportunity to learn and demonstrate their knowledge using their hands can help them to retain the information. Answers A and C are incorrect because although cross-curricular connections and choices can be effective supports, they are less directly targeted to math concept acquisition than hands-on work in this context. Answer B is incorrect because giving a student multiple tasks might be difficult if they are struggling with the first task.

44. D: Moving around the room and standing near students, even without saying a word, can help to minimize disruptive behaviors. This method, known as proximity control, allows teachers to attract student attention that might otherwise be directed toward their friends or other distractions. Students may also be more likely to ask for help if they can do so quietly, without having to ask in front of the class. Choice A is incorrect because clapping hands or blowing a whistle to get students' attention is not effective in managing student behaviors. This type of intervention adds to the noise and chaos it is intended to stop. Posting a written description of expected classroom behaviors can help to minimize unwanted behaviors, but writing is a form of verbal communication, so choice B is incorrect. Rewards may encourage good behavior from some students but are unlikely to affect the students prone to misbehavior, so choice C is incorrect.

45. C: Although all of these choices can be beneficial in supporting students like Max, it is important to distinguish the difference between accommodations and supplementing his curriculum. Providing opportunities for him to experience hands-on learning can be beneficial in allowing him to feel the numbers and improve his math. Accommodations are tools that allow him to access the same curriculum as his peers. Answer A is incorrect because although reading problems to him orally is beneficial, this is an accommodation to the general education curriculum. Answer B is incorrect because allowing him extra time would not supplement the curriculum. Answer D is incorrect because allowing him to use a computer can be helpful for an alternative curriculum or accommodation but not necessarily to supplement the curriculum.

46. C: Preventive strategies typically include what will be done in order to free students from the items or events that typically cause these behaviors. These may include removing a student from distractions or allowing them to run around the gym if they need it. These strategies can be used to help alleviate some of the behaviors once the triggers are determined. Answer A is incorrect because identifying the behaviors typically belongs in the "description of behavior" section of the plan. Answer B is incorrect because behaviors that serve a similar purpose as the unwanted behavior are called replacement behaviors. Answer D is incorrect because the instruction of individual skills falls under the category of teaching strategies.

47. A: In order to attain a measurable goal, there must be concrete evidence that the goal is or is not being met. Without this evidence, it is difficult to determine how much progress is being made and how much is left to accomplish. Goals that are measurable are crucial to refining exactly what it is that the goal is trying to achieve. Answer B is incorrect because a cost analysis is a component of an attainable goal. Answer C is incorrect because a clarified description may be beneficial for whether or not a goal is measurable, but it is more closely related to the specificity of the goal. Answer D is incorrect because overarching objectives are components of relevant goals.

48. B: This student has learned to perform the skills at home but has not generalized them to other settings. It is superfluous to reteach him the skills (A) because he has demonstrated their acquisition at home. Teaching skill maintenance (C) is unnecessary because the parents report he has performed the skills for years, so he has achieved maintenance but not generalization. Teaching skill discrimination (D) does not apply to this example as there was no mention of the student having any problems separating one skill or skill set from another or applying skills to the wrong tasks.

49. B: It is important for teachers to include needed classroom adaptations in their comprehensive plans for students with disabilities. Many of the classroom changes that teachers make are incidental but provide an immediate solution when they notice some students having difficulties; this is not rare (A). These kinds of changes are usually both necessary and appropriate, not the reverse (C). Therefore, they are likely to meet those students' needs, not unlikely (D). However, incidental modifications alone are insufficient. As teachers come to know individual students, they should plan adaptations for the needs they can predict before starting a lesson.

50. D: Multilevel instructional practices can be used in various grouping arrangements, including whole class (A), small group (B), and paired (C) contexts; no one of these is better than the others. When arrangements other than whole class instruction are used, the smaller groups of students are typically still mixed in character rather than being homogeneous. Multilevel instruction is based on the principle that all students have a chance to access suitable instruction and to get support from their teachers and classmates.

51. A: Read all answers; mark out any that are illogical. Next 'plug in' the remaining words and mark out those that are grammatically incorrect or do not sound right. Finally, think about context clues. Maze and Cloze tests are related. In a Cloze test, the reader uses context clues and familiar vocabulary to decide which words have been left out of a text. A Maze test supplies a number of possible answers and the reader must select the correct one. Possible answers can be syntactically possible but illogical, syntactically impossible but semantically plausible and both illogical and grammatically impossible.

52. B: Learning to learn is one of the most valuable skills or learning strategies for the real-world environment. It helps students understand how they learn, check their own progress, and adjust their strategies. When teachers lecture, students are often taught facts but are not taught how to incorporate the facts into real life situations. Using the strategy of learning to learn teaches students how to solve problems and think critically. Additionally, when this method is combined with group learning, students learn how to interact with others in a team environment, which enhances leadership skills. While repetition and memorization are useful strategies for learning, learning to learn aids in implementing the strategies that work for the student and the student's specific situation.

53. B: All students have different capabilities and capacities for learning, but teachers should not lower expectations for individuals based on perceived limitations or initial difficulties; doing so would unnecessarily limit or put pressure on individual students. If a majority of students are having difficulty with an assignment, they may need more scaffolding or teaching. Lowering expectations assumes students are incapable of success when they might have succeeded with more help. Making no changes will only result in students failing to finish the assignment or producing low quality work. Removing all expectations eliminates intentional instruction that is often required for students to progress.

54. C: RTI is a multi-tiered system in which a student with academic difficulties receives research-supported interventions and ongoing progress monitoring. If the student does not make adequate progress despite increasingly intensive interventions, this lack of response may indicate a possible learning disability.

55. B: Some of the children in Ms. Harris' class likely come from collectivist cultures. In America, individualism and competition are highly valued. In collectivist cultures, the good of the group and cooperation are more highly valued. Making these students work individually and not allowing them to work together or help each other would be at odds with their cultural backgrounds and values and would not be successful. Therefore, option A is incorrect.

Setting up collaborative learning groups who work together to complete a project would be congruent with these children's cultural mores and thus more likely to succeed. Therefore, option B is correct.

Allowing each student to teach class can be a valuable confidence booster in some circumstances. But in this case, many of the students would likely feel uncomfortable being in the spotlight as a result of being assigned a leadership role. These students' backgrounds tend to emphasize the importance of group identity over individual identity. Their cultures frown on the personal fame that is prized in American culture. Contributing to the collective public wellbeing is considered more honorable than individual identity in many cases. Therefore, option C is incorrect.

Some of the students in the classroom likely come from cultures that value cooperation above competition. In America, it is common for students to be encouraged, or even pushed, to strive for personal excellence and to be better than others. It is also common in American culture to publicize one's competitive success. Ms. Harris' students are likely to not agree with these practices. In their cultures, it is more common to sacrifice personal identity for the sake of the nation, the institution, or the family—i.e., the group. These students are more likely to feel pride in contributing to the whole than in standing out from the crowd. Therefore, option D is incorrect.

56. B: A sheltered workshop could be a good initial setting for a disabled individual to learn job skills if there is future transitioning. But in this option, Oscar would be assembling product sample kits, which involves multiple steps, and he would have only periodic group supervision. He would have trouble remembering all the steps and would be likely to stop working without more direct, continuous supervision. Therefore, option A is incorrect.

The warehouse packing job also has multiple steps, but in this option, Oscar would have one-on-one supervision with constant verbal prompts to complete each step. This would keep him on task. The repetition and constant reinforcement would help him learn a useful job skill. Packing is also larger-scale, more physical work than the seated manual work of assembling sample kits or applying labels. This is more suitable for Oscar as he has Down syndrome with low IQ scores and is normally passive. The combination of physical activity and using more gross motor skills than fine motor skills could benefit him. Therefore, option B is correct.

Applying labels is a repetitive task without many steps, so it could be easier. However, Oscar requires repeated prompts to stay on task. The classroom described would not afford him this; he would only get occasional prompts from the teacher, who has many students. And as a young adult, Oscar may not be able to stay in a classroom indefinitely. Therefore, option C is incorrect.

A class with only academic lessons and quizzes about job skills is not the most useful exercise for someone with Oscar's level of intellectual disabilities. He needs intensive training in actually doing a job to make a transition to real work. In his case, the real work would also need to be supervised on an ongoing basis. Therefore, option D is incorrect.

57. D: Having computers for every student is a good way to integrate technology into instruction. But excusing blind and visually impaired students from using the computers is not an example of appropriately integrating technology. Excusing the manually impaired student from typing is also not the best solution. Therefore option A is incorrect.

Reading to the visually impaired students and typing for the manually impaired student are two examples of poor use of technology in instruction and accommodating it to disabilities. It is also an inefficient use of Ms. Blanchard's time as she would not be able to work with the other students. Therefore option B is incorrect.

Giving an alternative recorded lesson to the visually impaired students is a waste of the computers. Hand-over-hand guidance is an intensive one-on-one activity that would prevent Ms. Blanchard from working with the other students. Therefore option C is incorrect.

Giving the visually impaired students speaking computers and earphones (so as not to disturb other students) is the best way to enable them to use computer technology without being able to see the screen. Giving the manually impaired student a touch screen enables him to use a computer without being able to type. Therefore option D is correct.

58. D: Assigning one student to compile and present the group's work could result in that student doing more of the project than the others. This would not be truly collaborative, so option A is incorrect.

Allowing students to volunteer to contribute to the project will result in some students doing most or all of the work while others end up doing little or none. This is not collaboration, so option B is incorrect.

The teacher leading the activity and directing what the students do would not be a collaborative group project. The students should be learning to cooperate with one another and to be more independent in conducting the project. The description in this option is a traditional teacher-led activity, so option C is incorrect.

Assigning each student an equal number of duties related to the project is a way to ensure that they all do equal amounts of work. The students will still be conducting the project themselves and working cooperatively together, but the teacher's initial assignment will prevent unequal distribution of participation, so option D is correct.

59. B: Although all of these choices may be beneficial in certain situations, it is most helpful to provide students with skeleton notes so they can keep up with the lecture and take notes. Many students with disabilities struggle to keep up with the pace of a typical lecture, so this strategy can allow them to understand the content and also write the notes. Note-taking is a valuable skill, so allowing them to practice it while also comprehending the lecture is valuable. Answer A is incorrect because simply giving them the entire presentation may overwhelm these students and create more work. Answer C is incorrect because giving them an exemption may cause them to lose focus or not pay attention to the lecture. Answer D is incorrect because it may not always be appropriate to have a partner during lecture time.

60. B: Although individualized instruction is helpful for many students, including students with a disability such as ADHD, it is the least effective of those listed for targeting the specific educational needs of students with ADHD. Many students with ADHD will simply need support in the classroom or in a separate setting that reduces opportunities for distraction. Strategies such as small-group instruction or separation from the rest of the class are more restrictive than the other options, so they should only be used when the IEP determines they are necessary. Instead, a teacher should seek to provide support within the student's primary class if possible. Answer A is incorrect because extra think time can allow students to collect their thoughts before they speak. Answer C is incorrect because settings with fewer distractions allow these students to concentrate. Answer D is incorrect because providing a model to demonstrate can allow the student to see how something is done before doing it.

61. A: Whiteboards can be very helpful for students who struggle with writing to determine whether or not they understand the lesson. These students have an opportunity to show what they learned by writing it in a fun way. It is important to check and see if students are understanding the material in a way that doesn't feel like they are being assessed. Answer B is incorrect because self-assessments may not always provide the best information on how a student is performing. Answer C is incorrect because cooperative learning would likely be more appropriate for larger groups of students. Answer D is incorrect because flip charts might be better suited for younger students who need visuals to learn.

62. C: Although all of these choices relate to science and can be functional for certain students, learning how to maintain a garden is the best example of a functional curriculum. A functional curriculum is designed to provide opportunities for students to work on their independent living skills. Maintaining a garden is a valuable skill that can be helpful for students like Brian to learn and apply once they graduate high school. The other answer choices are primarily academic and less tied to independent living or vocational skills.

63. B: Although it may be difficult to plan when she will be absent from school, it would be beneficial to Cheyenne to have someone such as her case manager support her in this task. Making up work on a regular basis can be difficult to do for anyone, especially an eighth grader with a disability. The case manager can help Cheyenne come up with a plan for working with her teachers and getting her assignments in. Answer A is incorrect because although it may be helpful to have Cheyenne talk to her teachers, it may be an overwhelming task. Answer C is incorrect because coming in before school might be helpful but only if it is arranged in advance with her teachers. Answer D is incorrect because giving her a deadline may overwhelm her and make it difficult for her to complete any of her work.

64. C: Although all these choices may be beneficial to students who struggle with organizational skills, data managers are the most effective in helping students organize tasks. These data managers allow students to put information on tasks into a system, and the system is instrumental in organizing it for them. Students with executive functioning skills can benefit from these tools in that they have to do less of the organization and management of information. Answer A is incorrect because FM listening devices are typically for students who struggle with hearing. Answer B is incorrect because speech recognition programs are designed for students who struggle with writing texts. Answer D is incorrect because abbreviation expanders are beneficial in helping students who may struggle with word processing.

65. A: Email writing is the most universally applicable lifelong writing skill among the options because it is used consistently across academic, professional, and personal contexts. Students will likely need support in the word usage and specifics of what to write in an email to various people. While essay writing, letter writing, and resume writing are also valuable skills, they are more context-specific or used less frequently across settings, making email writing the best answer given the emphasis on universal applicability.

66. D: Math simulation technology allows students to visualize problems that they are working on rather than just reading the text. This assistive technology can support students with math deficiencies in conceptualizing math problems and turning them into a visual as opposed to a standard written problem. This simulation allows the students to work through the same problem as the rest of the students. Answer A is incorrect because math simulation technology does more than simply allowing the students to recognize the text. Answer B is incorrect because although the technology may help the students write the problems, it is designed to allow them to conceptualize each problem. Answer C is incorrect because math simulation is also not designed to provide opportunities for the students to hear the text.

67. B: In order to allow for collaboration among students with and without disabilities, heterogeneous teams are likely to be most productive. In these groups, the teacher selects which students are in which groups in order to create a balance of ability levels among the students. This allows students with disabilities to have some success in working with students they may not always have the opportunity to work with. Answer A is incorrect because student-selected teams may leave some students with disabilities feeling left out because they were not chosen for a group. Answer C is incorrect because random teams may create an imbalance between students with and without disabilities in the class. Answer D is incorrect because homogeneous teams would group students based on ability, which would likely not make for the best balance in the class.

68. D: When teaching a science lesson to a group of third-grade students, it is important to incorporate hands-on learning activities. Learning centers can provide opportunities for these students to do activities and learn about different topics. Learning centers are most appropriate for younger students, such as a group of third graders. Answer A is incorrect because reciprocal teaching would be most appropriate for older students who are capable of teaching each other rather than younger students. Answer B is incorrect because Socratic questioning would be most appropriate for higher level questioning based on thoughtful dialogue between the teacher and student and is a skill that third graders likely would not have. Answer C is incorrect because direct instruction may be more appropriate for a more abstract topic such as reading or math, as it does not promote hands-on exploration and investigation.

69. C: Students with independent living skills goals will likely need some support in reaching their goals and will need to take it step by step. Researching ingredients is a great first step in knowing what is needed to make the meals. It is important that students are supported in their independent living skills goals while also being given a level of independence. Answer A is incorrect because just working in the cafeteria and cleaning likely will not prepare the student to cook a meal. Answer B is incorrect because shadowing at a restaurant may be fun for the student, but hands-on experiences are likely to be more beneficial. Answer D is incorrect because if students are making lunch each day, they likely do not need this goal.

70. D: While teacher collaboration is a recommended co-teaching practice, effective collaboration requires clearly defined, shared learning objectives. Without this, instruction could become inconsistent and support is less targeted. Both teachers need to be aligned in instructional strategies to increase the chances of student success. Answer A is incorrect because both teachers teaching as a team can be a great way to reach every student in the class. Answer B is incorrect because station teaching can be beneficial in that each teacher can teach to their strengths. Answer C is incorrect because it can be beneficial for one teacher to teach their area of specialty while the other teacher supports the students who are struggling.

71. A: When teaching students about study skills and how to use them, it is important to assist them in developing some methods that will work for them. Answer B is incorrect because independent practice would be difficult for students who are struggling to come up with ideas. Answer C is incorrect because developing a portfolio likely would be too much of a task to take on. Answer D is incorrect because although it may be beneficial, having a group discussion with the teacher's input is likely more beneficial in helping students develop successful study skills.

72. D: Providing students with many opportunities to read encourages reading proficiency by allowing them more reading practice. Providing the students with choices of reading materials (A) has also been shown to enhance their motivation to read because they have more control and choice than they do when reading only teacher-chosen materials, and because they can choose to read something that is personally appealing to them. When teachers can show students what is meaningful in what they read, students are more interested in reading (B). Teachers can also enhance students' motivation to read by making the activity fun (C).

73. A: The most accurate answer is choice A: Doing this helps Ms. Winslow's students to organize what they read and learn from the textbooks. While many of us are familiar with students never reading their textbooks (B), this is not Ms. Winslow's main reason for her practice. The textbook items she regularly points out to her students are all specific organizational devices. Thus, answer C is incorrect: This practice may or may not enhance her presentation, but it does facilitate learning. Answer D—that this helps students with learning disabilities but is a waste of time for other students—is also incorrect, since all students can benefit from being reminded to use these features in their textbooks as aids to effective learning.

74. C: Research has found that using writing as a tool for learning academic content is helpful to normally achieving students and students with learning disabilities (LD), so teaching students to avoid this (C) is not a recommendation. Based on their findings, researchers recommend teaching students to set specific, attainable goals for what they will write (A). They advise teachers to instruct students in strategies for planning what they will write, editing what they have written, and making indicated revisions (B). Researchers also recommend that teachers give LD students instruction in using PC word processing programs (D), which can make many aspects of writing much easier for them.

75. A: Jim's instruction can be considered quite effective, as he has not only scored 90% on classroom performance assessments and met or surpassed his IEP goals, but he has also increased his score on national norm-referenced standardized tests by 15% in a year. Scoring 20% below national norms does not indicate that his instruction is not effective enough (B). This is because norm-referenced tests are not useful for determining instructional effectiveness, as state and local teaching practices vary too much for the broad range of content on these tests to apply. Additionally, Jim has mild cognitive impairment and may or may not ever score equally with national averages. Because norm-referenced tests do not indicate instructional effectiveness, working on his instruction just to raise his scores on these tests (C) is unnecessary. More information is not needed (D) to know that he is demonstrating progress, so his instructional program must be working.

76. D: Summative assessments are given after instruction. Examples include tests at the ends of chapters, units, semesters, or terms; school district interim assessments or benchmark assessments; and standardized state tests. As such, they are often used to evaluate the effectiveness of instruction. Authentic assessments (A) are made in real-life situations, such as driver's license tests, or in simulations of real life. Ongoing assessments (B) are like formative assessments (C) in that they are made during instruction rather than after it. Formative assessments can be equated with practice that students receive as part of instruction, rather than scoring or grading what has already been learned as summative assessments do.

77. B: Curriculum-based measures are used in special education as quick, frequent assessments to determine whether or not students are making sufficient progress on their IEP goals. If a student with a specific learning disability falls behind on one of his or her IEP goals, the IEP team can review and implement measures to help the student before he or she falls too far behind. Choice A is incorrect because it refers to a type of norm-referenced test, where a student's scores are compared to similar students' scores. Choice C is incorrect because the most effective use of curriculum-based measures for a student with a specific learning ability is monitoring IEP progress, not general curriculum progress. Choice D is incorrect because curriculum-based measures do not always translate to official grades, as they are simply a progress-marking tool.

78. B: Reading comprehension and vocabulary cannot be sufficiently assessed with occasional, brief assessments. Performing continuous observation, using high-stakes and standardized testing, paying attention to grades, and closely tracking the outcomes of objective-linked assessments are interrelated tools that, when systematically organized, offer a thorough understanding of students' strengths and weaknesses.

79. C: A portfolio assessment is a purposeful collection of a student's various products showing what the student has done or made. It is possible to evaluate from these products what the student has learned and achieved. Therefore, option C is correct.

An authentic assessment is based on a demonstration of a skill or behavior in the context of real life. The description in this question is of classroom projects. Therefore, option A is incorrect.

A task analysis is a way of breaking down a complex task into smaller individual steps so a student may master one step at a time. One step is then connected to the next, and so on, until the student masters the whole task. The description in this question does not match that definition. Therefore, option B is incorrect.

A performance assessment is based on a student's performance of a behavior specified by the assessor. The teacher in this example has not specified that the students need to perform any particular behavior for her to assess. Therefore, option D is incorrect.

80. A: Johnny's IQ score places him in the gifted range. His rank is in the 97th percentile. This means that only 3 percent (the remainder of 100 percent minus 97 percent) of the population has a higher score than Johnny's. Therefore choice A is correct.

Johnny's score is at or above the scores of 97 percent of the population, not above only 96 percent. Only 3 percent, not 97 percent, of the population scored higher than Johnny. Therefore, choices B and C are incorrect.

The percentage of the population with an IQ score lower than or equal to Johnny's is 97 percent, not 3 percent. 3 percent of the population has a score higher than Johnny's, not lower. Therefore choice D is incorrect.

81. C: If these are IQ scores, Mario scored in the 99.99th percentile. This means he scored higher than all but 0.01% of the population. With an IQ score at the very top of the population, Mario would be considered gifted. Therefore, option C is correct.

These scores all express the same measures in different terms. Z-score, T-score, and scaled score express the same values as standard score, but they are based on a different numbering system. Based on the table's headings, these are not scores from different tests. Therefore, option A is incorrect.

Nothing in the table indicates that these scores represent different parts of a test. The table names different types of scoring methods. Therefore, option B is incorrect.

If these are IQ scores, Mario's score is higher than most of the population's. In addition to adaptive skills measures, the definition of intellectual disabilities is largely based on IQ scores. The mildest (highest IQ) level of intellectual disabilities corresponds to a range of IQ scores between 70 and 55. Mario's score is 155. Therefore, option D is incorrect.

82. C: Although all of these choices may be examples of some kind of formative assessment, observing her in class is most likely to provide the best data. Formative assessments are designed to assess what the student knows as the learning occurs. In order to monitor progress using formative assessments, it is important to take a look at the areas the student struggles in and if she is improving. Answer A is incorrect because interviewing a first grader like Andrea may not always provide the most accurate data. Answer B is incorrect because giving her academic probes would not show how she is developing on her overall social and behavioral skills as well as observation would. Answer D is incorrect because simply monitoring how she does on tests may not provide the whole picture in how she is developing overall.

83. B: One of the most productive strategies for students with disabilities is completing a portfolio. A portfolio allows the students to demonstrate what they know at the end of a unit or section. Summative assessments are designed to evaluate what a student has learned over a period of time and provide them with a grade. Answer A is incorrect because monitoring the students' IEP goals would be an example of a formative assessment. Answer C is incorrect because evaluation of students' continued eligibility is not used for grading or based on a particular unit. Answer D is incorrect because determining which accommodations students need is typically part of the IEP meeting.

84. D: Students that score below one standard deviation below the average level on an academic achievement test typically display a deficiency in that area. Because of this, a student like Jacob would likely need to be evaluated for special education services. The achievement test is just one piece of data that must be considered, and while Jacob's score likely shows a deficiency, one test alone is not enough to assume that he will be eligible for special education services. While more tests specific to written expression may occur at a later step, answer B is incorrect because the first step will most likely be evaluating Jacob for special education services. Answer C is incorrect because intelligence testing does not indicate whether or not a student has an academic skill deficiency.

85. A: Giving a student like Shamus a story starter and counting his correct writing sequences is one of the most beneficial curriculum-based assessments. This assessment focuses on many areas including spelling, punctuation, and content of the writing. Students that struggle with writing will often need practice writing short stories such as these, and it is easy to monitor their progress. Answer B is incorrect because simply giving him a list of spelling words only allows the teacher to focus on one area, spelling. Answer C is incorrect because curriculum-based assessments are not designed to take an entire class period. Answer D is incorrect because giving him a picture to write about might be more appropriate for a younger student.

86. A: A score of 100 on a standard IQ test indicates a score that is right in the middle of the average range when compared to other students his age. This indicates that Ricky's intelligence is where it is expected to be for someone his age. Additional assessments are necessary to determine whether he does or does not need special education services, however. Answer B is incorrect because a score of 100 is in the middle of the data, not an indication that he scored 100% on the test. Answer C is incorrect because additional assessments must be conducted to determine his need for services. Answer D is incorrect because Ricky may not need services, depending on the results of other assessments.

87. A: Although standardized tests can have many functions and be used in a variety of ways, they are designed to compare a student's score with what the average student scores. These can be beneficial in determining whether or not a student is keeping up with their peers in academic areas. Students with disabilities will often take the same standardized tests as their peers, but it is important to understand the areas that they struggle in and how to help them. Answer B is incorrect because progress is typically monitored through measures such as curriculum-based assessments. Answer C is incorrect because finding strengths and weaknesses in a student's development is an example of a developmental assessment. Answer D is incorrect because intellectual ability is typically measured using an IQ test.

88. D: Although all of these choices may provide instances to change the test or the format of the test, it is likely most beneficial to create a new test when the standards are modified. When students are unable to access the regular academic standards, it is often necessary to create a new assessment to meet the needs of these students and assess what they know. Although the majority of students can access these regular standards with accommodations or modifications, some students need to work with modified standards due to their disability. Answer A is incorrect because students who do not have access to the curriculum would likely not be assessed at all. Answer B is incorrect because students with intellectual disabilities may or may not be able to access the standards with accommodations or modifications. Answer C is incorrect because accommodated tests typically do not involve a new test being created.

89. A: Although all of these choices may be effective in certain situations, tally marks would likely be most beneficial in recording the number of outbursts. Tally marks can assist the teacher in determining the number of outbursts that the student has over a period of time. These tally marks can be used to identify when or where these outbursts are occurring and how they can be prevented. Answer B is incorrect because although time sampling can be helpful for certain student behaviors, outbursts are best measured using tally marks. Answers C and D involve qualitative data that are very useful for understanding the context and triggers of Matthew's outbursts, but they are time-consuming and harder to summarize numerically for frequent formative progress monitoring. Tally marks (frequency recording) give the teacher simple, countable data to track whether the number of outbursts is increasing or decreasing over time.

90. B: Norm-referenced tests can be helpful in comparing a student's score with a random sample of other students that are of the same age. This allows the evaluator to determine areas of strength and weakness for students by comparing them to others. It is important to understand where the average score stands when interpreting assessment results in order to determine appropriate instruction or programming. Answer A is incorrect because comparing a student's score to a previous score would be considered progress monitoring. Answer C is incorrect because it is important to consider where the standard deviation is when interpreting results, but the score cannot be compared to a standard deviation. Answer D is incorrect because these assessments compare all of the students, not just those with disabilities.

91. A: The purpose of an intelligence test is to measure a student's ability to reason and solve problems, which includes thinking abstractly. Intelligence tests can provide valuable information in deciphering the reasons that a student may struggle in particular areas. These tests can be beneficial for students of all grades and disabilities for gathering information. Answer B is incorrect because measuring a student's spoken language abilities would be considered a processing assessment. Answer C is incorrect because measuring a student's ability to convey ideas through oral language would be considered a communication assessment. Answer D is incorrect because visual information assessments would typically fall under the visual-spatial assessment categories.

92. C: A diagnostic assessment is used to identify a student's specific strengths and skill gaps so that meaningful, individualized IEP goals can be developed. Assessment data shows exactly which math problem-solving skills Peyton has mastered and which ones he still needs to learn. This information best guides his math instruction because the IEP team can write targeted goals. Answer A is incorrect because accommodations are determined through the IEP process, not by the diagnostic assessment alone. Answer B is incorrect because class placement is not the primary goal for Peyton. Answer D is incorrect because modifications are typically based on comprehensive IEP decisions, not diagnostic results alone.

93. C: Students who score in the below-average range on achievement tests with no other concerns will typically fall under the "specific learning disability" category. Students with specific learning disabilities have deficits in the areas of reading, writing, and math. It is important to understand the results of assessments in order to appropriately place students and provide services that the student will need. Answer A is incorrect because students with trouble in speech or communication would take a test specific to those needs. Answer B is incorrect because students who receive services under the other health impairment category will have a health impairment that impacts their access to education. Answer D is incorrect because a cognitive disability is not one of the disability categories under the Individuals with Disabilities Education Act.

94. D: Diagnostic assessments are used to determine what students already know in order to develop a curriculum. These kinds of tests include anything that is going to assess what the student's previous knowledge is before getting into the new content. This can be beneficial for students in special education in order to determine what interventions or supports they may need. Answer A is incorrect because pretests are a diagnostic that can be used to drive instruction. Answer B is incorrect because self-assessments can help the teacher understand what the student thinks of themselves and their skills. Answer C is incorrect because interviews can also be beneficial in understanding the needs of a student before designing the curriculum.

95. C: Although all of these choices might be beneficial to some students in improving behavior, observing her regularly can best help evaluate her behavior. If a student like Lisa is evaluated regularly, the causes of her behavior can be analyzed in order to guide instruction. It is important to constantly be thinking of new instructional practices and methods to support students with behavior struggles like Lisa. Answer A is incorrect because asking her to participate in class discussions might bring out more of the negative behavior that she tends to exhibit. Answer B is incorrect because although conferring with her might be somewhat beneficial, it is likely that her perception of issues will not lead to as meaningful changes as observing her actual behavior will. Answer D is incorrect because this would not be considered an assessment method but rather an instructional practice.

96. B: For students with specific learning disabilities, achievement tests are beneficial in gathering information about where the student may be deficient. Achievement tests such as the Wechsler

Individual Achievement Test correspond with the categories associated with specific learning disabilities. This information is valuable in assessment of where students need improvement and potential strategies for instruction. Answer A is incorrect because this kind of assessment would be more appropriate for a younger student who is new to school. Answer C is incorrect because this assessment is typically used for those students who are at least 16 years old. Answer D is incorrect because this kind of assessment is an intelligence test rather than an achievement test.

97. D: Professional development is not a trickle-down process but rather a collaboration of experts and teachers sharing research and experience. Answer A is not true because, although some principles of teaching are universal, a priority of professional development is to help the teachers where they are in order to help with site-specific needs. Answer B is not true because, although some professional development might be about classroom strategies, other types of professional development are definitely aimed at improving content knowledge. Answer C is not true because, like Answer A, although teachers should be aware of other opportunities in the field of education, a priority of professional development is to help the teacher with the job at hand.

98. C: While many laws are based on ethics, not all laws are ethical. Examples of what most would consider unethical laws include the Jim Crow laws in the United States that restricted the civil rights of black people or laws such as those imposed in Nazi Germany that permitted taking the lives and property of Jews. Answer A is correct in that laws are written, concrete, and enacted by people of authority. Answer B is correct in that ethics are a personal code enforced by a person's own conscience. Answer D is correct in that society transfers many of its ethics into laws to codify them.

99. B: Contacting the mother to see if Aaron missed his medication today would determine if his behavior was because of this, which is likely. Therefore, option B is correct.

Knowing that this student's mother has a history of sometimes having difficulty giving her son his medication, Mr. Love should act based on this information. Asking the doctor to raise the dosage would be inappropriate. Therefore, option A is incorrect.

Asking the principal to move Aaron to another class is not warranted under these circumstances. Since he does not usually display today's behavior in class, it is not likely due to his being in a class that does not meet his needs. Therefore, option C is incorrect.

Asking the doctor to consider a different drug is not indicated in this case. First Mr. Love needs to find out if Aaron received his medication today. Since today's behavior is atypical, there is no ongoing indication that his medication is ineffective. Since his mother sometimes misses giving Aaron his medication, this is the first possibility to investigate. Therefore, option D is incorrect.

100. C: A placement review committee consists of at least three members, two of whom are teachers. A teacher can refuse to participate on the committee. The committee conducts a thorough review of the student's behavior and makes a professional decision that considers both the needs of the student and the school. This committee must also take into consideration any disability the student might have, whether or not it is documented, and comply with the Americans with Disabilities Act, IDEA, and Section 504. While contacting the parents and speaking with the student are also good steps to take, a placement decision is decided by the placement review committee.

101. A: During the prereferral process, parents are not typically required to give their consent. This process typically consists of identifying areas in which the student struggles and developing strategies to assist this student. This may consist of interventions inside or outside of the classroom in addition to accommodations or modifications. Answer B is incorrect because it is important to collect data to determine whether or not a student is making sufficient progress. Answer C is incorrect because monitoring is important since it determines whether or not new strategies need to be implemented to better meet student needs. Answer D is incorrect because constantly evaluating the strategies and discussing them as a team is a necessary component of the prereferral process in meeting student needs.

102. B: Although all of these factors can have a significant impact on a student, the content the student has learned has the greatest impact on the special education identification process. Students may come from many different cultures and have learned different topics and ideas. The special education identification process will look at a student's progress and how much they know about certain subjects compared with their peers. Answer A is incorrect because although the language a student speaks is important, it does not necessarily correspond to whether or not they should receive special education services. Answer C is incorrect because knowing where a student comes from can be helpful, but it does not influence identification. Answer D is incorrect because religion also does not influence identification.

103. A: Documenting and explaining a student's educational/behavioral difficulties occur during the prereferral stage of the IEP process. Classroom accommodations and modifications are tested for effectiveness NOT after determining eligibility (B) for Special Education services, but during prereferral. The effectiveness of different instructional interventions is assessed NOT after IEP implementation (C) but during prereferral. Progress monitoring is done NOT only after IEP implementation (D) but also during prereferral. The IEP process steps are pre-referral, referral, identification, eligibility, IEP development, IEP implementation, and evaluation and reviews.

104. D: Planning for assistive services is not limited to OT and PT. All personnel who deliver services to the student should attend since they will need to know how the devices operate, so option A is incorrect.

OT, PT, direct care, and nurses should be informed, but so should others; therefore, option B is incorrect.

More than OT and nurses should attend. While doctors can provide information about the student's physical condition, many M.D.s do not attend these meetings because of various other demands on their time for medical services; therefore, option C is incorrect.

The personnel listed in this option, including the behavior specialist and teachers, will work directly with the student. They should have the information provided in the clinic and also have input regarding the student's educational needs and how these will impact planning for assistive technology; therefore, option D is correct.

105. B: Based on research findings, it is highly likely that Mr. Campbell was subject to the middle-class bias prevalent among middle-class teachers. Many lower-SES students appear to achieve less, but teacher expectations often have more influence on these results than student ability and/or performance. Therefore, option B is correct.

Because Mr. Leon came from a lower-SES background, he may identify with these students, but this does not necessarily mean he would inflate their grades. Applying insights from his own experience, he might just as likely avoid special favors, hoping to ensure the students' hard work and success in middle-class society. Therefore, option A is incorrect.

Undoubtedly these students feel more comfortable with Mr. Leon, and this could increase their motivation to succeed. But this is not the only reason for the difference. Their increased comfort and motivation may contribute to their improvement on objective measures but would not alone be enough to account for it. Removal of the middle-class bias would enable improved objective results and would also increase their comfort and motivation, which in turn could add to the improvement. Therefore, option C is incorrect.

These students probably did feel less comfortable with Mr. Campbell, but they may or may not have been underachieving in his class. The prevalence of middle-class bias among teachers would have an impact on their objective results regardless of the students' efforts. Therefore, option D is incorrect.

106. C: Joel has odd behaviors, but many can be remedied by training. A time-out is unlikely to change his behavior over the long term. Punishment is generally not the most effective method of changing behavior, especially if Joel has not yet been taught proper mealtime behavior; therefore, option A is incorrect.

Having Joel clean up the floor is another type of punishment. With an individual who has profound intellectual disabilities, this is unlikely to change his sitting and eating behavior; therefore, option B is incorrect.

The houseparent should meet with the IEP team to plan IEP objectives. The team can write objectives for Joel to sit facing forward with his legs under the table and to eat over the table. The behavior specialist can write a task analysis for the houseparent to implement in training him to perform these behaviors, with reinforcement of proper execution; therefore, option C is correct.

Placing a drop cloth under Joel's chair would make it easier for the houseparent to clean up after meals, but Joel will not learn anything. If he eats in other settings, he will still make a mess. If he learns to sit and eat properly at home, this will transfer to other places. It would be impractical and inappropriate to put a drop cloth under him wherever he eats; therefore, option D is incorrect.

107. C:

This program sounds like a good match for Pam, and she is interested in it. Foregoing the placement without attempting to work through the parents' misgivings would be unfairly denying her an opportunity for progress. Alternatively, placing her in the program regardless of her parents' fears could impede Pam's success by creating conflicting feelings in her. Her parents might make her feel guilty or pressure her not to continue. Her parents should also not be left to suffer with their anxiety. This makes answers A and B incorrect.

Pam and her parents should meet with the team from her previous placement and those in her new placement. Together, they can plan for a successful transition. The information and counseling both teams provide can allay her parents' fears, and all parties can provide input to help make the transition a smooth one; therefore, option C is correct.

A trial stay could be a good way for Pam and the staff to see how the placement might work out; however, given her parents' concerns about putting Pam into a new program, even a trial stay would be premature. Her parents might subsequently decide they want her to move out, creating a lot of instability and inconvenience for Pam and others. All involved parties should first meet to plan for the transition. Once adequate plans have been made and Pam's parents are informed and reassured by their daughter and staff, making them feel more comfortable with the change, it will be less likely or necessary that Pam's move would be only temporary; therefore, option D is incorrect.

108. B: James M. Baldwin used the term "mental deficiency" in 1901. In 1937, Tredgold referred to "a state of incomplete mental development," so option A is incorrect.

The criterion that intellectual disabilities originate during the developmental period, defined as from birth to age 16, was used by Heber for the AAMD's 1961 definition. It does not appear in earlier definitions, so option B is correct.

The association of intellectual disabilities with impaired adaptive behavior appears as early as 1937. In Tredgold's definition, he states "...that the individual is incapable of adapting himself to the normal environment of his fellows..." Therefore, option C is incorrect.

Contrary to Heber's 1961 AAMD definition, which states that intellectual disabilities originate in the developmental period, or Grossman's 1973 AAMD definition, which extends the developmental period to age 18, Edgar A. Doll's 1941 definition includes as one of his six criteria that intellectual disabilities "obtains at maturity." Therefore, option D is incorrect.

109. D: Although there may be many benefits to holding an externally facilitated IEP meeting, it typically takes a little longer for the special education teacher to prepare. The purpose of the externally facilitated IEP meeting is to include everyone in the conversation using an outside facilitator who may or may not know the student. The external facilitator will need to meet with the special education teacher beforehand in order to get an understanding of the student, which tends to take extra time. Answer A is incorrect because the facilitated IEP meeting is designed to be focused and handle one issue at a time. Answer B is incorrect because part of the facilitator's role is to ensure that they can problem solve whenever a conflict does arise. Answer C is incorrect because everyone on the IEP team will be included in the discussion at a facilitated IEP meeting.

110. C: Following evaluation, if a learning disability is identified, the school can only give Tran special education services with the written permission of his parents. Therefore, option C is correct.

An IQ test alone cannot be given because no single test can be used to identify a disability. All areas of any suspected disability must be evaluated. Therefore, option A is incorrect.

The Individuals with Disabilities Education Act (IDEA) 2004 stipulates that tests must be given in the child's native language, must measure a disability rather than limited English language skills, and must not discriminate on a racial or cultural basis. A reading test and writing test, both in English, would violate these rules. Therefore, option B is incorrect.

The school cannot write an IEP for Tran regardless of his test results. IDEA specifies that, to benefit from the educational program, Tran must be found to have a specific learning disability as well as a need for special education services. Following Tran's evaluation, a multidisciplinary team meeting should be held to develop an IEP. This meeting would include Tran's parents. Therefore, option D is incorrect.

111. C: Discussing the subject alone in the teacher's office during a free period would ensure the confidentiality of the conversation. Therefore, option C is correct.

Kim and her teacher should not discuss Kim's college applications in the hallway since they would be surrounded by other students, faculty, and staff. This disregards Kim's right to privacy. Therefore, option A is incorrect.

Discussing Kim's college applications in a small group session would expose the conversation to a few other students. This also does not respect her privacy. Therefore, option B is incorrect.

Discussing the subject in the general education classroom is not appropriate. Even though class has not yet begun, there are likely to be many other students already in the room. This would not be respecting Kim's privacy. Therefore, option D is incorrect.

112. D: It is part of the teacher's role to collaborate with community personnel in implementing Greg's IEP. Suggesting to the residential services program running Greg's group home that they install nonslip material on the tub floor and grab bars on the walls is a good idea. As Greg has showered many times before without falling, with these safeguards in place he could continue to shower independently, but with less risk of slipping and falling again. This would be safer for Greg's wellbeing and would also probably relieve a lot of his father's anxiety. Therefore, option D is correct.

Advising a more restrictive placement is a step backward. Greg is young, and since his father approves of his current placement, he should be allowed as much independence as possible. Therefore, option A is incorrect.

Counseling Greg's father to accept the injury is irresponsible. Though it is true that accidents do happen in life, in this case Greg's disabilities include a poor sense of balance. Thus, the odds of his falling are greater than those of a person with a normal sense of balance, and some precautions should be taken. Therefore, option B is incorrect.

In this kind of placement, it has already been determined that Greg is capable of taking a shower without group home staff directly supervising him. They were following his IEP objectives for personal care, so an investigation is unnecessary and inappropriate since they were not negligent. Therefore, option C is incorrect.

113. D: To integrate Stewart into a classroom with no other wheelchairs, personnel should make sure that the room is wheelchair-accessible and that Stewart can navigate in the room. They should also instruct the other students how to avoid such things as tripping over footrests, accidentally kicking Stewart, bumping into his chair, getting their feet run over, blocking Stewart's path, and so forth. As long as accommodations are made in terms of the room's physical arrangement and everybody learns how to behave around a wheelchair, Stewart can be integrated into the classroom. Therefore, option D is correct.

To advise against the placement goes against the policy of inclusion. A student in a wheelchair has the right to be integrated into the general education classroom if he has the ability to participate in the educational activities of that class. Therefore, option A is incorrect.

Transferring Stewart from his wheelchair to a regular student desk and back again is unrealistic and impractical. It would require help, which might not be available. It would also be more restrictive. Staying in his wheelchair, Stewart has mobility in and out of the classroom, but if he cannot transfer between the wheelchair and another chair on his own, he will be dependent on somebody else to help him. Therefore, option B is incorrect.

Limiting Stewart's placement to only classes with other students in wheelchairs is not the least restrictive environment. Additionally, such a class may not be available. Or, even if there are other classes with students in wheelchairs, those classes may not be the most appropriate to Stewart's educational needs. Therefore, option C is incorrect.

114. A: The Education for All Handicapped Children Act of 1975 established that children with disabilities must be provided free appropriate public education (FAPE). This law became the basis for all special education funding and services through the federal government. The establishment of

FAPE was important for students with disabilities and continues to be today. Answer B is incorrect because grants to states to fund special education programs had already been established prior to the passage of this act. Answer C is incorrect because school-to-work facilitation legislation was passed after 1975. Answer D is incorrect because the inclusion of all students with disabilities in statewide testing also occurred after the passage of this legislation.

115. C: Students in elementary school do not typically attend their IEP meetings. These students are often too young to attend and understand the discussion at the meeting, so they are most often not invited to the meeting. It is important to understand a student's maturity level before inviting him or her to an important meeting to discuss the IEP. Answer A is incorrect because the school psychologist can be an important member of the IEP team for students with emotional disturbances in writing behavior plans or monitoring goals. Answer B is incorrect because the director of special education is also often invited to these IEP meetings. Answer D is incorrect because most school districts require a building administrator to attend IEP meetings as well.

116. D: Although removing the student from the school is certainly an option, this is not typically one of the dispute-resolution processes. These processes are designed for parents to work through disputes that they may have with their child's IEP in order to find a solution. Removing the student from the school likely would not solve the problem with regard to the IEP. Answer A is incorrect because parents and stakeholders have the right to file a complaint with the Department of Education if they choose to. Answer B is incorrect because asking for mediation can be a beneficial way to seek a compromise in regard to the IEP. Answer C is incorrect because parents can also file a due process complaint if the other two strategies prove to be unsuccessful.

117. D: According to the Family Educational Rights and Privacy Act, parents have the right to access testing protocols that are used to evaluate students for special education services. These protocols are considered educational records and part of the student's file. Because of this, the Family Educational Rights and Privacy Act requires that school personnel make these available to parents upon request. Answer A is incorrect because only teachers and staff that work directly with the student have access to that student's IEP. Answer B is incorrect because parents have the right to review and inspect previous IEPs that they may not have copies of. Answer C is incorrect because once an IEP from a prior year is finalized and becomes part of the student's educational record, it cannot be amended. Only the current IEP may be amended through appropriate procedures.

118. D: Although special education teachers have a variety of roles and responsibilities, facilitating 504 plans is typically not one of them. These plans are often administered by the school counselors or building administrators. Although it is possible that special education teachers are involved in this process in some capacity, it is typically not the expectation. Answer A is incorrect because communicating student accommodations to general education teachers is a crucial responsibility of the special education teacher. Answer B is incorrect because the special education teacher is typically responsible for assisting in developing the schedule for paraprofessionals. Answer C is incorrect because special education teachers often team-teach lessons with general education teachers to ensure the instruction is differentiated.

119. B: Although it is possible that the occupational therapist would provide services to a student with a hearing impairment, this is not typically the case. Occupational therapists often provide support to students who struggle with motor skills in the school setting. Students with hearing impairments may or may not have these needs, and it is important to understand the areas in which students have needs in order to consult with the appropriate service providers. Answer A is incorrect because speech-language pathologists typically assist students with hearing impairments in working on communication skills. Answer C is incorrect because the school nurse is an important member of the team in determining the health care services that the student may need at school. Answer D is incorrect because the audiologist typically conducts the hearing screening to determine the impact of the hearing impairment.

120. B: Although all of these choices may be involved in the MTSS process in some capacity, it is most likely that the special education teacher discusses which students may need to be evaluated for special education services. The MTSS process is designed to provide general education support for students who may be struggling academically, socially, or emotionally. The special education teacher is typically involved in this process to provide input on students who may not be responding appropriately to these interventions and need to be evaluated for special education services. Answer A is incomplete because, while MTSS is a general education framework that supports all students (including those with disabilities), the special education teacher's primary unique role in MTSS meetings is to help the team consider students who may require a special education evaluation. Answer C is incorrect because the special education teacher typically is not the individual responsible for providing these general education interventions. Answer D is incorrect because although it may be possible that students who exit special education are discussed through the MTSS process, it is more often designed for students who have yet to be evaluated.